The Easy

Ninja Foodi

PossibleCooker

COOKBOOK for Beginners

Michayuela Svoyibodova

2000 Days of Quick, Tasty and Effortless Recipes
Book with Step-by-Step Cooking Tips for
Every Meal of the Day

TABLE OF CONTENTS

INTRODUCTION

Welcome to the Ninja Foodi PossibleCooker Cookbook, where culinary possibilities are limitless! In a world where time is often a luxury, the Ninja Foodi PossibleCooker steps in as your reliable kitchen partner, designed to simplify meal preparation without compromising flavor or quality. This innovative appliance combines multiple cooking methods into one sleek, powerful unit, allowing you to pressure cook, slow cook, sauté, steam, bake, roast, and air fry with ease. If you're ready to explore a new realm of cooking and discover how the PossibleCooker can transform your culinary adventures, you've come to the right place!

Embracing Versatility

The Ninja Foodi PossibleCooker is not just another kitchen gadget; it's a complete cooking solution. Imagine the convenience of making a hearty, comforting beef stew in the pressure cooker mode, then seamlessly transitioning to bake a batch of fresh, warm muffins, all in the same pot. This versatility means that you can prepare everything from quick weeknight dinners to elaborate weekend feasts with minimal effort and cleanup.

One of the standout features of the PossibleCooker is its ability to deliver results that rival those of traditional cooking methods, yet in a fraction of the time. Pressure cooking tenderizes meats and infuses flavors, while slow cooking allows for

deep, rich tastes to develop over hours. The air frying function provides that satisfying crunch without the excess oil, making it easier to enjoy your favorite comfort foods without the guilt. This appliance adapts to your cooking style, making it suitable for everything from busy families to culinary adventurers who love to experiment with new flavors.

With this cookbook, you'll learn to maximize the potential of your Ninja Foodi. Each recipe is designed to take advantage of the appliance's unique features, ensuring that your meals are not only easy to make but also packed with flavor. The beauty of the PossibleCooker lies in its ability to simplify the cooking process while delivering delicious results. No more juggling multiple pots and pans or worrying about cooking times; with the PossibleCooker, you can streamline your kitchen experience and enjoy more time with family and friends.

Culinary Adventures Await

One of the joys of cooking is the opportunity to explore diverse cuisines and flavors. The Ninja Foodi PossibleCooker Cookbook invites you on a culinary adventure that spans the globe, bringing together recipes inspired by various traditions and cultures. Whether you're in the mood for classic Italian pasta dishes, spicy Mexican tacos, or comforting American casseroles, this cookbook has you covered.

Each recipe is crafted with accessibility in mind, allowing cooks of all skill levels to create mouthwatering meals. You'll find a wide variety of recipes, including appetizers, main courses, side dishes, and even desserts. We aim to provide something for everyone, from those seeking to impress guests at a dinner party to families looking for a nutritious meal that can be made in a hurry. Our recipes are structured to highlight the best qualities of the PossibleCooker, ensuring that every dish is not only delicious but also achievable.

Throughout this cookbook, you will encounter recipes that highlight seasonal ingredients, encouraging you to utilize what's fresh and available in your local market. This approach not only enhances flavor but also supports sustainable eating practices. Cooking with seasonal ingredients can lead to more vibrant and nourishing meals while promoting local farmers and producers. We believe that food should be celebrated, and what better way to do that than by using the best ingredients nature has to offer?

Cooking with Purpose

At the heart of this cookbook is a desire to inspire you to cook with purpose. Preparing meals for yourself and your loved ones can be a rewarding experience, fostering connection and creating cherished memories. As you delve into the recipes, we encourage you to embrace the process of cooking as a means of nurturing relationships and celebrating special moments.

Cooking is not just about feeding the body; it's about nourishing the soul. Each meal presents an opportunity to express love and creativity, whether it's a simple weeknight dinner shared with family or a lavish holiday feast for friends. The meals you create can bring people together in meaningful ways, and we hope to ignite your passion for cooking.

This cookbook is filled with stories and anecdotes that celebrate the joy of cooking and the bonds formed around the dinner table. As you gather your ingredients and prepare the recipes, take a moment to appreciate the connections food can create. Remember, cooking is as much about the experience as it is about the end result.

Simple and Delicious Recipes

In today's busy world, finding time to prepare healthy, delicious meals can be a challenge. The Ninja Foodi PossibleCooker Cookbook offers a collection of recipes that are not only quick and easy but also packed with flavor. We understand that you may be juggling work, family, and personal commitments, so we've created recipes that cater to your busy lifestyle without sacrificing taste.

Expect to find a variety of one-pot meals that minimize cleanup while maximizing flavor. From comforting soups and stews to zesty stir-fries and crispy air-fried snacks, our recipes are designed to be both satisfying and convenient. Each recipe includes preparation and cooking times, ensuring you can plan your meals effectively. We've also included meal prep ideas and batch cooking tips, allowing you to plan ahead and make the most of your cooking time.

You'll appreciate the straightforward instructions, which guide you through each step of the cooking process, making it easier for you to create restaurant-quality dishes in your own kitchen. Additionally, we've incorporated time-saving tips, such as using pre-chopped vegetables and pantry staples, to help streamline your cooking experience. With the Ninja Foodi, delicious meals are always within reach, no matter how busy your schedule may be.

Join the Culinary Community

As you embark on this culinary journey with the Ninja Foodi PossibleCooker Cookbook, remember that you are part of a vibrant community of home cooks who share a passion for good food. We encourage you to connect with fellow Ninja Foodi enthusiasts, share your creations, and celebrate the joy of cooking together.

Social media platforms and online forums are brimming with home cooks eager to share their experiences, tips, and adaptations of recipes. Engaging with this community can enhance your cooking skills and inspire you to try new techniques and flavors. By sharing your culinary successes and even your missteps, you contribute to a culture of learning and growth.

With each recipe you try, you're not just making a meal; you're creating an experience, one that you can share with others. So, gather your ingredients, unleash your creativity, and prepare to elevate your cooking to new heights. The Ninja Foodi PossibleCooker is your gateway to culinary exploration, where every dish is a possibility, and every meal is a celebration.

Final Thoughts

In conclusion, the Ninja Foodi PossibleCooker Cookbook is more than just a collection of recipes; it's an invitation to embark on a culinary adventure. As you explore the recipes within these pages, remember that cooking is an art that evolves with each experience. The Ninja Foodi PossibleCooker provides the tools to enhance your culinary journey, enabling you to create delectable dishes that bring joy to your table. Let's cook, create, and celebrate the beauty of good food together!

Chapter 1

Breakfasts

Chapter 1 Breakfasts

Nutmeg-Spiced Pumpkin Custard

Prep time: 15 minutes | Cook time: 6 to 7 hours | Serves 8

- ¼ cup melted butter, divided
- 2½ cups canned pumpkin purée
- 2 cups coconut milk
- 4 eggs
- 1 tablespoon pure vanilla extract
- 1 cup almond flour
- ½ cup granulated erythritol
- 2 ounces (57 g) protein powder
- 1 teaspoon baking powder
- 1 teaspoon ground cinnamon
- ¼ teaspoon ground nutmeg
- Pinch ground cloves

1. Lightly grease the insert of the Ninja Foodi PossibleCooker with 1 tablespoon of the butter. 2. In a large bowl, whisk together the remaining butter, pumpkin, coconut milk, eggs, and vanilla until well blended. 3. In a small bowl, stir together the almond flour, erythritol, protein powder, baking powder, cinnamon, nutmeg, and cloves. 4. Add the dry ingredients to the wet ingredients and stir to combine. 5. Pour the mixture into the insert. 6. Cover and cook on low for 6 to 7 hours. 7. Serve warm.

"Baked" Oatmeal

Prep time: 10 minutes | Cook time: 2½ to 3 hours | Serves 4 to 6

- ⅓ cup oil
- ½ cup sugar
- 1 large egg, beaten
- 2 cups dry quick oats
- 1½ teaspoons baking powder
- ½ teaspoon salt
- ¾ cup milk

1. Pour the oil into the Ninja Foodi PossibleCooker, making sure to grease the bottom and sides evenly. 2. Add the remaining ingredients to the Ninja Foodi PossibleCooker and stir thoroughly until well mixed. 3. Cover and cook on low for 2½ to 3 hours, or until the mixture reaches your desired consistency.

Savory Bacon and Egg Casserole

Prep time: 15 minutes | Cook time: 5 to 6 hours | Serves 8

- 1 tablespoon bacon fat or extra-virgin olive oil
- 12 eggs
- 1 cup coconut milk
- 1 pound (454 g) bacon, chopped and cooked crisp
- ½ sweet onion, chopped
- 2 teaspoons minced garlic
- ¼ teaspoon freshly ground black pepper
- ⅛ teaspoon salt
- Pinch red pepper flakes

1. Lightly grease the insert of the Ninja Foodi PossibleCooker with the bacon fat or olive oil. 2. In a medium bowl, whisk together the eggs, coconut milk, bacon, onion, garlic, pepper, salt, and red pepper flakes. Pour the mixture into the Ninja Foodi PossibleCooker. 3. Cover and cook on low for 5 to 6 hours. 4. Serve warm.

Mediterranean Egg Bake

Prep time: 10 minutes | Cook time: 5 to 6 hours | Serves 4

- 1 tablespoon extra-virgin olive oil
- 12 eggs
- ½ cup coconut milk
- ½ teaspoon dried oregano
- ½ teaspoon freshly ground black pepper
- ¼ teaspoon salt
- 2 cups chopped spinach
- 1 tomato, chopped
- ¼ cup chopped sweet onion
- 1 teaspoon minced garlic
- ½ cup crumbled goat cheese

1. Lightly grease the insert of the Ninja Foodi PossibleCooker with the olive oil. 2. In a large bowl, whisk together the eggs, coconut milk, oregano, pepper, and salt, until well blended. 3. Add the spinach, tomato, onion, and garlic, and stir to combine. 4. Pour the egg mixture into the insert and top with the crumbled goat cheese. 5. Cover and cook on low 5 to 6 hours, until it is set like a quiche. 6. Serve warm.

Creamy Carrot Cake Oatmeal

Prep time: 10 minutes | Cook time: 6 hours | Serves 8

- 4½ cups water
- 1 (20-ounce / 567-g) can crushed pineapple, undrained
- 2 cups shredded carrots
- 1 cup steel-cut oats
- 1 cup raisins
- 2 teaspoons ground cinnamon
- 1 teaspoon pumpkin pie spice
- Brown sugar (optional)

1. In a 4-quart Ninja Foodi PossibleCooker coated with cooking spray, combine the first seven ingredients. Cover and cook on low for 6 to 8 hours or until oats are tender and liquid is absorbed. Sprinkle with brown sugar if desired.

Zucchini-Carrot Bread

Prep time: 15 minutes | Cook time: 3 to 5 hours | Makes 8 slices

- 2 teaspoons butter, for greasing pan
- 1 cup almond flour
- 1 cup granulated erythritol
- ½ cup coconut flour
- 1½ teaspoons baking powder
- 1 teaspoon ground cinnamon
- ½ teaspoon ground nutmeg
- ½ teaspoon baking soda
- ¼ teaspoon salt
- 4 eggs
- ½ cup butter, melted
- 1 tablespoon pure vanilla extract
- 1½ cups finely grated zucchini
- ½ cup finely grated carrot

1. Begin by lightly greasing a 9-by-5-inch loaf pan with butter and set it aside. 2. Place a small rack in the bottom of your Ninja Foodi PossibleCooker to elevate the loaf pan. 3. In a large bowl, mix together the almond flour, erythritol, coconut flour, baking powder, cinnamon, nutmeg, baking soda, and salt until evenly combined. 4. In a separate medium bowl, whisk the eggs, melted butter, and vanilla extract until smooth and well blended. 5. Pour the wet ingredients into the dry ingredients, stirring until combined. 6. Fold in the shredded zucchini and carrot, mixing until evenly distributed. 7. Spoon the batter into the prepared loaf pan, spreading it out evenly. 8. Place the loaf pan on the rack inside the Ninja Foodi PossibleCooker, cover, and cook on high for 3 hours, or until a toothpick inserted into the center comes out clean. 9. Once cooked, remove the loaf pan from the Ninja Foodi PossibleCooker, let the bread cool completely, then slice and serve.

Savory Breakfast Sausage Loaf

Prep time: 10 minutes | Cook time: 3 hours | Serves 8

- 1 tablespoon extra-virgin olive oil
- 2 pounds (907 g) ground pork
- 2 eggs
- 1 sweet onion, chopped
- ½ cup almond flour
- 2 teaspoons minced garlic
- 2 teaspoons dried oregano
- 1 teaspoon dried thyme
- 1 teaspoon fennel seeds
- 1 teaspoon freshly ground black pepper
- ½ teaspoon salt

1. Lightly grease the insert of the Ninja Foodi PossibleCooker with the olive oil. 2. In a large bowl, stir together the pork, eggs, onion, almond flour, garlic, oregano, thyme, fennel seeds, pepper, and salt until well mixed. 3. Transfer the meat mixture to the Ninja Foodi PossibleCooker's insert and shape it into a loaf, leaving about ½ inch between the sides and meat. 4. Cover, and if your Ninja Foodi PossibleCooker has a temperature probe, insert it. 5. Cook on low until it reaches an internal temperature of 150°F (66°C), about 3 hours. 6. Slice in any way you prefer and serve.

Polenta

Prep time: 10 minutes | Cook time:2 to 9 hours | Serves 8 to 10

- 4 tablespoons melted butter, divided
- ¼ teaspoon paprika
- 6 cups boiling water
- 2 cups dry cornmeal
- 2 teaspoons salt

1. Use 1 tablespoon of butter to lightly grease the inside of the Ninja Foodi PossibleCooker, then sprinkle the paprika inside. Set the Ninja Foodi PossibleCooker to the high setting. 2. Add the remaining ingredients to the Ninja Foodi PossibleCooker in the order listed, including the additional 1 tablespoon of butter. Stir well to combine. 3. Cover and cook on high for 2 to 3 hours or on low for 6 to 9 hours, stirring occasionally to prevent sticking. 4. Once cooked, pour the hot polenta into two lightly greased loaf pans. Allow the polenta to chill in the refrigerator for at least 8 hours or overnight until firm. 5. To serve, cut the chilled polenta into ¼-inch-thick slices. In a large nonstick skillet, melt 2 tablespoons of butter over medium heat, then add the polenta slices. Cook until browned on one side, then flip to brown the other side. 6. For a breakfast option, serve with your choice of sweetener or toppings.

Maple Granola

Prep time: 20 minutes | Cook time: 2 hours | Makes 5 to 6 cups

- ¾ cup extra-virgin olive oil, plus more for Ninja Foodi PossibleCooker
- 4 cups old-fashioned rolled oats
- 1 cup raw shelled pistachios, almonds, walnuts, pecans, or hazelnuts, chopped if large
- ¼ cup packed brown sugar
- ½ teaspoon ground cinnamon
- ½ teaspoon coarse salt
- ½ cup pure maple syrup
- 1 tablespoon vanilla extract
- ½ cup dried apricots, dates, cherries, figs, raisins, blueberries, or cranberries, chopped if large

1. Lightly brush the insert of a 5- to 6-quart Ninja Foodi PossibleCooker with oil and preheat the cooker. 2. In the Ninja Foodi PossibleCooker, mix together the oats, nuts, brown sugar, cinnamon, and ¼ teaspoon salt until well combined. Add the oil, maple syrup, and vanilla, stirring until everything is evenly coated. Increase the heat to high and partially cover by turning the lid 45 degrees to allow moisture to escape. Cook on high for about 2 hours, stirring every 30 minutes until the mixture is golden brown and toasted (do not cook on low). After 1 hour, rotate the Ninja Foodi PossibleCooker insert to help prevent scorching. 3. Once toasted, stir in the dried fruit, then spread the granola in a single layer on a rimmed baking sheet to cool completely. If desired, sprinkle with the remaining ¼ teaspoon salt. Store the granola in an airtight container at room temperature for up to 1 week.

Enchiladas Verde

Prep time: 20 minutes | Cook time: 4 to 5 hours | Serves 6 to 8

- 2 tablespoons vegetable oil
- 1 medium onion, finely chopped
- 1 Anaheim chile pepper, seeded and finely chopped
- 4 tablespoons finely chopped fresh cilantro
- 3 cups tomatillo salsa
- ½ cup chicken broth
- 2½ cups finely shredded mild Cheddar cheese
- 2 cups finely shredded Monterey Jack or Pepper Jack cheese
- 2 cups crumbled queso fresco
- 2 cups sour cream
- 12 (6-inch) round white or yellow corn tortillas, cut in strips or roughly torn

1. Begin by coating the insert of a 5- to 7-quart Ninja Foodi PossibleCooker with nonstick cooking spray, or line it with a slow-cooker liner according to the manufacturer's directions. 2. In a medium saucepan over medium-high heat, warm the oil. Add the onion and chile, sautéing until softened and fragrant, about 3 to 5 minutes. 3. Stir in 2 tablespoons of cilantro, the salsa, and broth, allowing the mixture to simmer for 30 minutes, or until slightly reduced and thickened. Remove from heat and let cool slightly. In a mixing bowl, combine the Cheddar and Monterey Jack cheese. 4. In a separate bowl, mix together the queso fresco, remaining 2 tablespoons of cilantro, and sour cream until well combined. 5. Spread a thin layer of the sauce on the bottom of the Ninja Foodi PossibleCooker insert. Layer one-third of the tortillas evenly over the sauce in the bottom of the Ninja Foodi PossibleCooker. 6. Spread half of the queso fresco mixture over the tortillas, followed by one-third of the shredded cheese. Repeat the layering with tortillas, sauce, queso fresco mixture, and shredded cheese. Finish with the remaining tortillas, sauce, and shredded cheese on top. 7. Cover and cook on low for 3 to 4 hours, or until the casserole is heated through and the cheese is bubbling. Remove the cover and cook for an additional 30 to 45 minutes to allow the top to set. 8. Serve directly from the Ninja Foodi PossibleCooker set on warm to keep the dish at the perfect temperature.

Homemade Crunchy Granola

Prep time: 15 minutes | Cook time: 4 hours | Makes 8 cups

- Nonstick cooking spray
- 4 cups old-fashioned rolled oats
- 1 cup slivered almonds
- 1 cup coarsely chopped pecans
- 1 cup sunflower seeds
- 1 cup shredded coconut
- ⅓ cup butter or coconut oil
- 2 tablespoons safflower oil
- ½ cup honey
- ⅓ cup brown sugar
- 2 teaspoons vanilla
- 1 teaspoon ground cinnamon
- ½ teaspoon salt

1. Spray the Ninja Foodi PossibleCooker with the nonstick cooking spray. 2. In the Ninja Foodi PossibleCooker, combine the oats, almonds, pecans, sunflower seeds, and coconut. 3. In a medium saucepan over low heat, heat the butter, safflower oil, honey, brown sugar, vanilla, cinnamon, and salt until the butter melts, about 5 minutes. 4. Drizzle the butter mixture over the ingredients in the Ninja Foodi PossibleCooker and stir to coat. 5. Cover, but leave the lid slightly ajar, and cook on low for 3 to 4 hours, stirring every hour if possible, until the mixture is golden brown. 6. Remove the granola to greased baking sheets and spread into an even layer. Let cool, and then break into pieces. Serve or store in an airtight container at room temperature.

Pumpkin Spice Breakfast Bars

Prep time: 15 minutes | Cook time: 3 hours | Makes 8 bars

Crust:

- 5 tablespoons butter, softened, divided
- ¾ cup unsweetened

Filling:

- 1 (28-ounce / 794-g) can pumpkin purée
- 1 cup heavy (whipping) cream
- 4 eggs
- 1 ounce (28 g) protein powder
- 1 teaspoon pure vanilla

- shredded coconut
- ½ cup almond flour
- ¼ cup granulated erythritol

- extract
- 4 drops liquid stevia
- 1 teaspoon ground cinnamon
- ½ teaspoon ground ginger
- ¼ teaspoon ground nutmeg
- Pinch ground cloves
- Pinch salt

Make the Crust: 1. Lightly grease the bottom of the insert of the Ninja Foodi PossibleCooker with 1 tablespoon of the butter. 2. In a small bowl, stir together the coconut, almond flour, erythritol, and remaining butter until the mixture forms into coarse crumbs. 3. Press the crumbs into the bottom of the insert evenly to form a crust. Make the Filling: 4. In a medium bowl, stir together the pumpkin, heavy cream, eggs, protein powder, vanilla, stevia, cinnamon, ginger, nutmeg, cloves, and salt until well blended. 5. Spread the filling evenly over the crust. 6. Cover and cook on low for 3 hours. 7. Uncover and let cool for 30 minutes. Then place the insert in the refrigerator until completely chilled, about 2 hours. 8. Cut into squares and store them in the refrigerator in a sealed container for up to 5 days.

Keto Granola

Prep time: 10 minutes | Cook time: 3 to 4 hours | Serves 16

- ½ cup coconut oil, melted
- 2 teaspoons pure vanilla extract
- 1 teaspoon maple extract
- 1 cup chopped pecans
- 1 cup sunflower seeds
- 1 cup unsweetened shredded

- coconut
- ½ cup hazelnuts
- ½ cup slivered almonds
- ¼ cup granulated erythritol
- ½ teaspoon cinnamon
- ¼ teaspoon ground nutmeg
- ¼ teaspoon salt

1. Lightly grease the insert of the Ninja Foodi PossibleCooker with 1 tablespoon of coconut oil. 2. In a large bowl, whisk together the remaining coconut oil, vanilla, and maple extract. Add the pecans, sunflower seeds, coconut, hazelnuts, almonds, erythritol, cinnamon, nutmeg, and salt, tossing until the nuts and seeds are fully coated. 3. Pour the mixture into the greased Ninja Foodi PossibleCooker insert. 4. Cover and cook on low for 3 to 4 hours, stirring occasionally, until the granola becomes crispy. 5. Once done, transfer the granola to a baking sheet lined with parchment or foil and allow it to cool completely. 6. Store the cooled granola in a sealed container in the refrigerator for up to 2 weeks.

Creamy Dulce de Leche Spread

Prep time: 5 minutes | Cook time: 2 hours | Makes 2½ cups

- 2 (14-ounce / 397-g) cans sweetened condensed milk
- Cookies, for serving

1. Place unopened cans of milk in Ninja Foodi PossibleCooker. Fill cooker with warm water so that it comes above the cans by 1½ to 2 inches. 2. Cover cooker. Cook on high 2 hours. 3. Cool unopened cans. 4. When opened, the contents should be thick and spreadable. Use as a filling between 2 cookies.

Welsh Rarebit

Prep time: 10 minutes | Cook time: 1½ to 2½ hours | Serves 6 to 8

- 1 (12-ounce / 340-g) can beer
- 1 tablespoon dry mustard
- 1 teaspoon Worcestershire sauce
- ½ teaspoon salt
- ⅛ teaspoon black or white pepper
- 1 pound (454 g) American

- cheese, cubed
- 1 pound (454 g) sharp Cheddar cheese, cubed
- English muffins or toast
- Tomato slices
- Bacon, cooked until crisp
- Fresh steamed asparagus spears

1. In a Ninja Foodi PossibleCooker, combine the beer, mustard, Worcestershire sauce, salt, and pepper. Cover and cook on high for 1 to 2 hours, or until the mixture begins to boil. 2. Gradually add the cheese, stirring constantly, allowing each portion to melt completely before adding more. 3. Once all the cheese has melted, continue heating on high for an additional 20 to 30 minutes, uncovered, stirring frequently to ensure a smooth texture. 4. Serve the hot cheese mixture over toasted English muffins or toasted bread cut into triangles. Garnish with tomato slices, strips of crispy bacon, and steamed asparagus spears for added flavor and presentation.

Creamy Nut and Coconut Breakfast Delight

Prep time: 10 minutes | Cook time: 8 hours | Serves 6

- 1 tablespoon coconut oil
- 1 cup coconut milk
- 1 cup unsweetened shredded coconut
- ½ cup chopped pecans
- ½ cup sliced almonds
- ¼ cup granulated erythritol
- 1 avocado, diced
- 2 ounces (57 g) protein powder
- 1 teaspoon ground cinnamon
- ¼ teaspoon ground nutmeg
- ½ cup blueberries, for garnish

1. Lightly grease the insert of a slower cooker with the coconut oil. 2. Place the coconut milk, shredded coconut, pecans, almonds, erythritol, avocado, protein powder, cinnamon, and nutmeg in the Ninja Foodi PossibleCooker. 3. Cover and cook on low for 8 hours. 4. Stir the mixture to create the desired texture. 5. Serve topped with the blueberries.

Huevos Rancheros

Prep time: 10 minutes | Cook time: 3 hours | Serves 8

- 1 tablespoon extra-virgin olive oil
- 10 eggs
- 1 cup heavy (whipping) cream
- 1 cup shredded Monterey Jack cheese, divided
- 1 cup prepared or homemade salsa
- 1 scallion, green and white parts, chopped
- 1 jalapeño pepper, chopped
- ½ teaspoon chili powder
- ½ teaspoon salt
- 1 avocado, chopped, for garnish
- 1 tablespoon chopped cilantro, for garnish

1. Begin by coating the Ninja Foodi PossibleCooker insert lightly with olive oil to prevent sticking. 2. In a large mixing bowl, whisk together the eggs, heavy cream, ½ cup of cheese, salsa, chopped scallion, jalapeño, chili powder, and salt until well combined. Pour this mixture into the greased Ninja Foodi PossibleCooker, then evenly sprinkle the remaining ½ cup of cheese over the top. 3. Cover the Ninja Foodi PossibleCooker and cook on low for about 3 hours, or until the eggs are set and firm. 4. Allow the cooked eggs to cool slightly before slicing into wedges. Serve each piece garnished with fresh avocado slices and a sprinkle of cilantro for a bright, fresh finish.

Buttery Coconut Bread

Prep time: 10 minutes | Cook time: 3 to 4 hours | Makes 8 slices

- 1 tablespoon butter, softened
- 6 large eggs
- ½ cup coconut oil, melted
- 1 teaspoon pure vanilla extract
- ¼ teaspoon liquid stevia
- 1 cup almond flour
- ½ cup coconut flour
- 1 ounce (28 g) protein powder
- 1 teaspoon baking powder

1. Grease an 8-by-4-inch loaf pan with butter to prevent sticking. 2. In a medium bowl, whisk together the eggs, oil, vanilla, and stevia until fully blended. 3. In a separate small bowl, combine the almond flour, coconut flour, protein powder, and baking powder, mixing until evenly distributed. 4. Gradually add the dry ingredients to the wet ingredients, stirring until well combined. 5. Pour the batter into the prepared loaf pan, then place the pan on a rack inside the Ninja Foodi PossibleCooker. 6. Cover and cook on low for 3 to 4 hours, or until a knife inserted into the center of the bread comes out clean. 7. Allow the bread to cool in the loaf pan for 15 minutes before removing it and transferring it to a wire rack to cool completely. 8. Store the cooled bread in an airtight container in the refrigerator for up to 1 week.

Cinnamon Nut Streusel Cake

Prep time: 10 minutes | Cook time: 3 to 4 hours | Serves 8 to 10

- 1 (16-ounce / 454-g) package pound cake mix, prepared according to package directions
- ¼ cup packed brown sugar
- 1 tablespoon flour
- ¼ cup chopped nuts
- 1 teaspoon cinnamon

1. Liberally grease and flour a 2-pound (907-g) coffee can, or Ninja Foodi PossibleCooker baking insert, that fits into your Ninja Foodi PossibleCooker. Pour prepared cake mix into coffee can or baking insert. 2. In a small bowl, mix brown sugar, flour, nuts, and cinnamon together. Sprinkle over top of cake mix. 3. Place coffee tin or baking insert in Ninja Foodi PossibleCooker. Cover top of tin or insert with several layers of paper towels. 4. Cover cooker itself and cook on high 3 to 4 hours, or until toothpick inserted in center of cake comes out clean. 5. Remove baking tin from Ninja Foodi PossibleCooker and allow to cool for 30 minutes before cutting into wedges to serve.

Dill-Asparagus Bake

Prep time: 10 minutes | Cook time: 4 to 5 hours | Serves 8

- 1 tablespoon extra-virgin olive oil
- 10 eggs
- ¾ cup coconut milk
- ½ teaspoon salt
- ¼ teaspoon freshly ground
- black pepper
- 2 teaspoons chopped fresh dill
- 2 cups chopped asparagus spears
- 1 cup chopped cooked bacon

1. Lightly grease the insert of the Ninja Foodi PossibleCooker with olive oil. 2. In a medium bowl, whisk together the eggs, coconut milk, salt, pepper, and dill until well combined. Stir in the asparagus and bacon. Pour the egg mixture into the prepared Ninja Foodi PossibleCooker. 3. Cover and cook on low for 4 to 5 hours, until the eggs are set. 4. Serve warm for the best flavor.

Three-Cheese Veggie Strata Bake

Prep time: 20 minutes | Cook time: 6 hours | Serves 2

- 1 tablespoon extra-virgin olive oil
- 1 tablespoon butter
- 1 onion, chopped
- 2 garlic cloves, minced
- 1½ cups baby spinach leaves
- 1 red bell pepper, chopped
- 1 large tomato, seeded and chopped
- 1 cup cubed ham
- Nonstick cooking spray
- 5 eggs, beaten
- 1 cup milk
- ½ teaspoon salt
- ½ teaspoon dried thyme leaves
- ⅛ teaspoon freshly ground black pepper
- 6 slices French bread, cubed
- 1 cup shredded Cheddar cheese
- ½ cup shredded Swiss cheese
- ¼ cup grated Parmesan cheese

1. In a medium saucepan over medium heat, heat the olive oil and butter. Add the onion and garlic, and sauté, stirring, until tender, about 6 minutes. 2. Add the spinach and cook until wilted, about 5 minutes. Remove from the heat and add the bell pepper, tomato, and ham. 3. Line the Ninja Foodi PossibleCooker with heavy-duty foil and spray with the nonstick cooking spray. 4. In a medium bowl, beat the eggs, milk, salt, thyme, and black pepper well. 5. In the Ninja Foodi PossibleCooker, layer half of the French bread. Top with half of the vegetable and ham mixture, and sprinkle with half of the Cheddar and Swiss cheeses. Repeat the layers. 6. Pour the egg mixture over everything, and sprinkle with the Parmesan cheese. 7. Cover and cook on low for 6 hours, or until the temperature registers 160ºF (71ºC) on a food thermometer and the mixture is set. 8. Using the foil sling, remove from the Ninja Foodi PossibleCooker, and serve.

Breakfast Fruit Compote

Prep time: 5 minutes | Cook time: 2 to 7 hours | Serves 8 to 9

- 1 (12-ounce / 340-g) package dried apricots
- 1 (12-ounce / 340-g) package pitted dried plums
- 1 (11-ounce / 312-g) can mandarin oranges in light
- syrup, undrained
- 1 (29-ounce / 822-g) can sliced peaches in light syrup, undrained
- ¼ cup white raisins
- 10 maraschino cherries

1. Place all ingredients in the Ninja Foodi PossibleCooker and stir until well combined. 2. Cover the Ninja Foodi PossibleCooker with the lid. Cook on low for 6 to 7 hours, or on high for 2 to 3 hours, until the dish is fully cooked and flavors are blended.

Southwest Breakfast Casserole

Prep time: 10 minutes | Cook time: 8 hours | Serves 2

- 1 teaspoon butter, at room temperature, or extra-virgin olive oil
- 2 eggs
- 2 egg whites
- 1 teaspoon ground cumin
- 1 teaspoon smoked paprika
- ⅛ teaspoon sea salt
- Freshly ground black pepper
- ½ cup shredded pepper Jack cheese
- ½ cup canned fire-roasted diced tomatoes
- ½ cup canned black beans, drained and rinsed
- 1 teaspoon minced garlic
- 3 corn tortillas
- ¼ cup fresh cilantro, for garnish

1. Begin by coating the inside of the Ninja Foodi PossibleCooker generously with butter to prevent sticking. 2. In a small bowl, whisk together the eggs, egg whites, cumin, paprika, salt, and a few turns of freshly ground black pepper until well blended. 3. In another bowl, mix together the cheese, chopped tomatoes, black beans, and minced garlic. 4. Layer the ingredients: Place one corn tortilla at the base of the Ninja Foodi PossibleCooker, then add half of the cheese and bean mixture over it. Pour one-third of the egg mixture over the cheese and beans, then layer with another tortilla. Repeat by adding the rest of the cheese and bean mixture, followed by another third of the egg mixture. Place the final tortilla on top and pour the remaining egg mixture over it. 5. Cover and cook on low for approximately 8 hours, or overnight, allowing flavors to blend and set. Garnish with fresh cilantro just before serving for a bright, fresh finish.

Crustless Wild Mushroom–Kale Quiche

Prep time: 10 minutes | Cook time: 5 to 6 hours | Serves 8

- 1 tablespoon extra-virgin olive oil
- 12 eggs
- 1 cup heavy (whipping) cream
- 1 tablespoon chopped fresh thyme
- 1 tablespoon chopped fresh chives
- ¼ teaspoon freshly ground black pepper
- ⅛ teaspoon salt
- 2 cups coarsely chopped wild mushrooms (shiitake, portobello, oyster, enoki)
- 1 cup chopped kale
- 1 cup shredded Swiss cheese

1. Begin by lightly greasing the inside of the Ninja Foodi PossibleCooker with olive oil to prevent sticking. 2. In a medium bowl, whisk together the eggs, heavy cream, thyme, chives, salt, and pepper until well combined. Gently fold in the mushrooms and kale, ensuring they are evenly distributed. Pour this mixture into the greased Ninja Foodi PossibleCooker, and sprinkle the cheese evenly over the top. 3. Cover and cook on low for 5 to 6 hours, until the eggs are set and the dish is cooked through. 4. Serve the dish warm for the best flavor and texture.

Summer Squash and Mushroom Strata

Prep time: 20 minutes | Cook time: 6 hours | Serves 2

- 1 onion, chopped
- 2 garlic cloves, minced
- 1½ cups sliced cremini mushrooms
- 1 red bell pepper, chopped
- 1 yellow summer squash, chopped
- Nonstick cooking spray
- 6 slices French bread, cubed
- 1 cup shredded Cheddar cheese
- 1 cup shredded Swiss cheese
- 5 eggs, beaten
- 1 cup milk
- 1 tablespoon Dijon mustard
- ½ teaspoon salt
- ½ teaspoon dried basil leaves
- ⅛ teaspoon freshly ground black pepper

1. In a medium bowl, combine the chopped onion, garlic, mushrooms, bell pepper, and squash, mixing until well blended. 2. Lightly spray the inside of the Ninja Foodi PossibleCooker with nonstick cooking spray to prevent sticking. 3. Begin layering the ingredients in the Ninja Foodi PossibleCooker: start with a layer of bread, followed by a portion of the vegetable mixture, and sprinkle with both Cheddar and Swiss cheeses. 4. In a separate medium bowl, whisk together the eggs, milk, mustard, salt, basil, and pepper until fully combined. 5. Carefully pour the egg mixture over the layers in the Ninja Foodi PossibleCooker, ensuring it evenly covers the bread and vegetables. 6. Cover the Ninja Foodi PossibleCooker and cook on low for about 6 hours, or until the internal temperature reaches 160ºF (71ºC) on a food thermometer. 7. Once cooked, cut the casserole into squares and serve warm.

Savory Sausage and Cheese Quiche

Prep time: 20 minutes | Cook time: 6 hours | Serves 2

- 8 ounces (227 g) pork sausage
- 1 onion, chopped
- 1 cup sliced mushrooms
- Nonstick baking spray containing flour
- 2 garlic cloves, minced
- 1 red bell pepper, chopped
- 1 cup shredded Cheddar cheese, divided
- 4 eggs, beaten
- 1 cup whole milk
- ½ cup all-purpose flour
- ½ teaspoon baking powder
- ½ teaspoon salt
- ½ teaspoon dried basil leaves
- ⅛ teaspoon freshly ground black pepper
- ⅓ cup grated Parmesan cheese

1. In a medium saucepan over medium heat, cook the sausage with the onions, stirring to break up the meat, until the sausage is browned, about 10 minutes. Drain well and add the mushrooms; cook, stirring, until the mushrooms give up their liquid and the liquid evaporates, about 5 minutes. 2. Line the Ninja Foodi PossibleCooker with heavy-duty foil. Spray the foil with the nonstick baking spray containing flour. 3. In the Ninja Foodi PossibleCooker, layer the sausage mixture, garlic, and bell pepper. Top with ½ cup of Cheddar cheese. 4. In a medium bowl, beat the eggs, milk, flour, baking powder, salt, basil, and pepper. Pour the egg mixture into the Ninja Foodi PossibleCooker and top with the remaining ½ cup of Cheddar cheese. Sprinkle with the Parmesan cheese. 5. Cover and cook on low for 6 hours, or until the quiche registers 160ºF (71ºC) on a food thermometer, the edges are browned, and the center is set. 6. Remove from the Ninja Foodi PossibleCooker and let stand for 5 minutes; cut into wedges and serve.

Creamy Pumpkin-Pecan Breakfast Bowl

Prep time: 10 minutes | Cook time: 8 hours | Serves 4

- 1 tablespoon coconut oil
- 3 cups cubed pumpkin, cut into 1-inch chunks
- 2 cups coconut milk
- ½ cup ground pecans
- 1 ounce (28 g) plain protein powder
- 2 tablespoons granulated erythritol
- 1 teaspoon maple extract
- ½ teaspoon ground nutmeg
- ¼ teaspoon ground cinnamon
- Pinch ground allspice

1. Lightly grease the insert of a slower cooker with the coconut oil. 2. Place the pumpkin, coconut milk, pecans, protein powder, erythritol, maple extract, nutmeg, cinnamon, and allspice in the insert. 3. Cover and cook on low for 8 hours. 4. Stir the mixture or use a potato masher to create your preferred texture, and serve.

Creamy Overnight Oatmeal with Cinnamon Sugar

Prep time: 5 minutes | Cook time: 3 to 10 hours | Serves 8

- 3¾ cups old-fashioned rolled oats
- 8 cups water
- ½ teaspoon salt
- 4 tablespoons (½ stick)
- unsalted butter, cut into small pieces
- 2 cups milk or cream, warmed, for serving
- ¼ cup cinnamon sugar for serving

1. Coat the insert of a 5- to 7-quart Ninja Foodi PossibleCooker with nonstick cooking spray or line the insert with a slow-cooker liner according to manufacturer's directions. 2. Combine the oatmeal, water, and salt in the cooker. Cover and cook on low for 8 to 10 hours or on high for 3 to 4 hours, until the oats are creamy. Stir in the butter. Serve with warmed milk and cinnamon sugar.

Breakfast Hominy

Prep time: 5 minutes | Cook time: 8 hours | Serves 5

- 1 cup dry cracked hominy
- 1 teaspoon salt
- Black pepper (optional)
- 3 cups water
- 2 tablespoons butter

1. In a greased Ninja Foodi PossibleCooker, combine all ingredients, stirring well to ensure even mixing. 2. Cover the Ninja Foodi PossibleCooker and set it to cook on low for 8 hours, or let it cook overnight for a ready-to-eat breakfast. 3. Serve warm in the morning, perfect for a cozy start to the day.

Cinnamon Blueberry Apple Compote

Prep time: 10 minutes | Cook time: 3 hours | Serves 10 to 12

- 1 quart natural applesauce, unsweetened
- 2 Granny Smith apples, unpeeled, cored, and sliced
- 1 pint fresh or frozen blueberries
- ½ tablespoon ground cinnamon
- ½ cup pure maple syrup
- 1 teaspoon almond flavoring
- ½ cup walnuts, chopped
- Nonfat cooking spray

1. Stir together applesauce, apples, and blueberries in Ninja Foodi PossibleCooker sprayed with nonfat cooking spray. 2. Add cinnamon and maple syrup. 3. Cover. Cook on low 3 hours. 4. Add almond flavoring and walnuts just before serving.

Chapter 2

Beans and Grains

Chapter 2 Beans and Grains

South Indian Sambar with Mixed Vegetables and Pigeon Peas

Prep time: 20 minutes | Cook time: 4½ to 6½ minutes | Serves 6

Sambar Masala:

- 1 teaspoon rapeseed oil
- 3 tablespoons coriander seeds
- 2 tablespoons split gram
- 1 teaspoon black
- peppercorns
- ½ teaspoon fenugreek seeds
- ½ teaspoon mustard seeds
- ¼ teaspoon cumin seeds
- 12 whole dried red chiles

Sambar:

- 1½ cups split yellow pigeon peas, washed
- 2 fresh green chiles, sliced lengthwise
- 2 garlic cloves, chopped
- 6 pearl onions
- 4 to 5 tablespoons sambar masala
- 2 teaspoons salt
- 1 to 2 carrots, peeled and chopped
- 1 red potato, peeled and diced
- 1 white radish (mooli), peeled and chopped into 2¾-inch sticks
- 1 tomato, roughly chopped
- 4 cups water
- 2 to 3 moringa seed pods, or ⅓ pound (151 g) green beans or asparagus, chopped into 2¾-inch lengths
- 2 tablespoons tamarind paste
- ½ teaspoon asafetida
- 2 teaspoons coconut oil
- 1 teaspoon mustard seeds
- 20 curry leaves
- 2 dried red chilies
- Handful fresh coriander leaves, chopped (optional)

Make the Sambar Masala: 1. Add the oil to a medium nonstick skillet. Add all of the remaining ingredients and roast for a few minutes until fragrant. The spices will brown a little, but don't let them burn. 2. Remove from the heat and pour onto a plate to cool. Once cooled, place into your spice grinder or mortar and pestle and grind to a powder. Set aside. Make the Sambar: 3. Heat the Ninja Foodi PossibleCooker to high and add the pigeon peas, green chiles, garlic, pearl onions, sambar masala, salt, carrots, potatoes, radish, tomato, and water. 4. Cover and cook for 4 hours on high, or for 6 hours on low. 5. Add the moringa (or green beans or asparagus), tamarind paste, and asafetida. Cover and cook for another 30 minutes. 6. When you're ready to serve, heat the coconut oil in a frying pan and pop the mustard seeds with the curry leaves and dried chiles. Pour over the sambar. Top with coriander leaves (if using) and serve.

Spiced Split Chickpeas with Turnips

Prep time: 10 minutes | Cook time: 4 to 7 hours | Serves 6

- 2 teaspoons cumin seeds, divided
- 1 teaspoon mustard seeds
- 1 teaspoon coriander seeds
- 1 tablespoon rapeseed oil
- 1½-inch piece cassia bark
- 4 small turnips, peeled and chopped
- 1 cup dried split chickpeas, washed
- 4 cups hot water
- 3 ripe tomatoes, chopped
- finely
- 1 or 2 fresh green chiles, chopped
- 1½-inch piece fresh ginger, grated
- 1 small onion, sliced
- 2 garlic cloves, sliced
- ½ teaspoon turmeric
- 1 teaspoon salt
- ½ teaspoon chili powder
- Handful fresh coriander leaves, chopped

1. Preheat the Ninja Foodi PossibleCooker on high. 2. Place 1 teaspoon of the cumin seeds, and the mustard, and coriander seeds in a dry frying pan and roast until they turn a shade darker and become fragrant. Crush the spices in a mortar and pestle or a spice grinder. 3. Add the oil to the Ninja Foodi PossibleCooker and heat. Then add the cassia bark and the remaining cumin seeds and cook for a few moments. 4. Put the turnips, split chickpeas, and water into the Ninja Foodi PossibleCooker. Then add the tomatoes, green chiles, ginger, onion, and garlic. Stir in the turmeric, salt, chili powder, and ground spices. 5. Cook on high for 4 hours, or on low for 6 hours. If you want to thicken the dhal, remove the lid and cook on high for another 30 minutes to 1 hour. 6. Once soft and cooked through, add the chopped coriander leaves.

Barbecue Baked Beans

Prep time: 10 minutes | Cook time: 3 to 4 hours | Serves 8 to 10

- 2 (16-ounce / 454-g) cans baked beans, your choice of variety
- 2 (15-ounce / 425-g) cans kidney or pinto beans, or one of each, drained
- ½ cup brown sugar
- 1 cup ketchup
- 1 onion, chopped

1. Combine all ingredients in Ninja Foodi PossibleCooker. Mix well. 2. Cover and cook on low 3 to 4 hours, or until heated through.

Spicy Bean Medley

Prep time: 10 minutes | Cook time: 3 to 4 hours | Serves 8 to 10

- 1 (16-ounce / 454-g) can kidney beans, drained
- 1 (15-ounce / 425-g) can lima beans, drained
- ¼ cup vinegar
- 2 tablespoons molasses
- 2 heaping tablespoons brown sugar
- 2 tablespoons minced onion
- Mustard to taste
- Tabasco sauce to taste

1. Place beans in Ninja Foodi PossibleCooker. 2. Combine remaining ingredients. Pour over beans. 3. Cover. Cook on low 3 to 4 hours.

Pizza Beans

Prep time: 30 minutes | Cook time: 7 to 9 hours | Serves 6

- 1 (16-ounce / 454-g) can pinto beans, drained
- 1 (16-ounce / 454-g) can kidney beans, drained
- 1 (2¼-ounce / 64-g) can ripe olives sliced, drained
- 1 (28-ounce / 794-g) can stewed or whole tomatoes
- ¾ pound (340 g) bulk Italian sausage
- 1 tablespoon oil
- 1 green pepper, chopped
- 1 medium onion, chopped
- 1 garlic clove, minced
- 1 teaspoon salt
- 1 teaspoon dried oregano
- 1 teaspoon dried basil
- Parmesan cheese

1. In the Ninja Foodi PossibleCooker, combine the beans, olives, and tomatoes, mixing well. 2. In a skillet, heat a bit of oil over medium heat and brown the sausage until fully cooked. Drain the sausage, reserving the drippings in the skillet, and transfer the sausage to the Ninja Foodi PossibleCooker. 3. Using the reserved drippings, sauté the green pepper for about 1 minute, stirring constantly. Add the onions and cook, stirring, until they start to turn translucent. Add the garlic and cook for an additional minute. Transfer this mixture to the Ninja Foodi PossibleCooker. 4. Stir in your choice of seasonings, ensuring everything is well combined. 5. Cover the Ninja Foodi PossibleCooker and cook on low for 7 to 9 hours, allowing the flavors to meld together. 6. Serve warm, topped with a sprinkle of Parmesan cheese for added flavor.

Herb-Infused Rice

Prep time: 5 minutes | Cook time: 4 to 6 hours | Serves 6

- 3 chicken bouillon cubes
- 3 cups water
- 1½ cups long-grain rice, uncooked
- 1 teaspoon dried rosemary
- ½ teaspoon dried marjoram
- ¼ cup dried parsley, chopped
- 1 tablespoon butter or margarine
- ¼ cup onions, diced
- ½ cup slivered almonds (optional)

1. Mix together chicken bouillon cubes and water. 2. Combine all ingredients in Ninja Foodi PossibleCooker. 3. Cook on low 4 to 6 hours, or until rice is fully cooked.

Kidney Beans

Prep time: 15 minutes | Cook time: 6 to 7 hours | Serves 12

- 2 (30-ounce / 850-g) cans kidney beans, rinsed and drained
- 1 (28-ounce / 794-g) can diced tomatoes, drained
- 2 medium red bell peppers, chopped
- 1 cup ketchup
- ½ cup brown sugar
- ¼ cup honey
- ¼ cup molasses
- 1 tablespoon Worcestershire sauce
- 1 teaspoon dry mustard
- 2 medium red apples, cored, cut into pieces

1. Add all ingredients, except for the apples, to the Ninja Foodi PossibleCooker and stir to combine. 2. Cover the Ninja Foodi PossibleCooker and cook on low for 4 to 5 hours, allowing the flavors to blend. 3. After this time, add the apples to the Ninja Foodi PossibleCooker and stir them into the mixture. 4. Cover again and cook on low for an additional 2 hours, or until the apples are tender.

Basil and Pine Nut Pilaf

Prep time: 10 minutes | Cook time: 2½ hours | Serves 8 to 10

- 2 tablespoons unsalted butter
- 1 cup pine nuts
- 3 cups converted white rice
- 4½ to 5½ cups chicken or vegetable broth
- 1 teaspoon freshly ground black pepper
- ½ cup finely chopped fresh basil, plus additional whole leaves, for garnish

1. Prepare a 5- to 7-quart Ninja Foodi PossibleCooker by coating the insert with nonstick cooking spray or lining it with a slow-cooker liner, following the manufacturer's instructions. 2. In a small sauté pan over medium-high heat, melt the butter. Add the pine nuts and sauté, stirring occasionally, until they begin to turn golden, about 4 minutes. Remove from heat and set aside. 3. In the Ninja Foodi PossibleCooker, combine the rice, 4½ cups of broth, and black pepper, stirring to mix. Cover and cook on high for 1 hour. 4. After 1 hour, stir in the toasted pine nuts and chopped basil, then re-cover and continue cooking for an additional 1½ hours, or until the rice is tender and the liquid has been absorbed. 5. Serve the rice directly from the Ninja Foodi PossibleCooker set to warm, garnishing with whole basil leaves for a fresh finish.

Earthy Whole Brown Lentil Dhal

Prep time: 10 minutes | Cook time: 6 to 8 hours | Serves 6

- 6⅓ cups hot water
- 2 cups whole brown lentils
- 1 tablespoon ghee
- 1 teaspoon freshly grated ginger
- 1 teaspoon sea salt
- 1 teaspoon turmeric
- 7 to 8 ounces (198 to 227 g)
- canned tomatoes
- 4 garlic cloves, finely chopped
- 1 or 2 fresh green chiles, finely chopped
- 1 onion, chopped
- 1 teaspoon garam masala
- Handful fresh coriander leaves, chopped

1. Rinse the lentils thoroughly under cold water, then set them aside to drain. 2. Preheat the Ninja Foodi PossibleCooker on high. Add the drained lentils along with all other ingredients, except for the garam masala and fresh coriander leaves. Stir everything together to combine well. 3. Cover the Ninja Foodi PossibleCooker and cook on high for 6 hours, or set to low and cook for 8 hours, until the lentils are soft and flavors are well blended. 4. Just before serving, stir in the garam masala and garnish with fresh coriander leaves for added flavor. Serve warm and enjoy.

Smoky Beans

Prep time: 20 minutes | Cook time: 4 to 6 hours | Serves 10 to 12

- 1 large onion, chopped
- 1 pound (454 g) ground beef, browned
- 1 (15-ounce / 425-g) can pork and beans
- 1 (15-ounce / 425-g) can ranch-style beans, drained
- 1 (16-ounce / 454-g) can kidney beans, drained
- 1 cup ketchup
- 1 teaspoon salt
- 1 tablespoon prepared mustard
- 2 tablespoons brown sugar
- 2 tablespoons hickory-flavored barbecue sauce
- ½ to 1 pound (227 to 454 g) small smoky link sausages (optional)

1. In a skillet over medium heat, brown the ground beef with the onion until fully cooked, then drain off any excess fat. Transfer the beef and onion mixture to a Ninja Foodi PossibleCooker set on high. 2. Add all remaining ingredients to the Ninja Foodi PossibleCooker and stir thoroughly to combine. 3. Switch the Ninja Foodi PossibleCooker to low and cook for 4 to 6 hours, allowing the flavors to meld. Before serving, use a paper towel to carefully blot any excess oil from the surface, then stir and serve warm.

Lotsa-Beans Ninja Foodi PossibleCooker Casserole

Prep time: 30 minutes | Cook time: 3 to 4 hours | Serves 15 to 20

- 8 bacon strips, diced
- 2 onions, thinly sliced
- 1 cup packed brown sugar
- ½ cup cider vinegar
- 1 teaspoon salt
- 1 teaspoon ground mustard
- ½ teaspoon garlic powder
- 1 (28-ounce / 794-g) can baked beans
- 1 (16-ounce / 454-g) can
- kidney beans, rinsed and drained
- 1 (15½-ounce / 439-g) can pinto beans, rinsed and drained
- 1 (15-ounce / 425-g) can lima beans, rinsed and drained
- 1 (15½-ounce / 439-g) can black-eyed peas, rinsed and drained

1. Cook bacon in skillet until crisp. Remove to paper towels. 2. Drain, reserving 2 tablespoons drippings. 3. Sauté onions in drippings until tender. 4. Add brown sugar, vinegar, salt, mustard, and garlic powder to skillet. Bring to boil. 5. Combine beans and peas in Ninja Foodi PossibleCooker. Add onion mixture and bacon. Mix well. 6. Cover. Cook on high 3 to 4 hours.

Savory Spicy Black Beans with Root Vegetables

Prep time: 20 minutes | Cook time: 8 hours | Serves 2

- 1 onion, chopped
- 1 leek, white part only, sliced
- 3 garlic cloves, minced
- 1 jalapeño pepper, minced
- 2 Yukon Gold potatoes, peeled and cubed
- 1 parsnip, peeled and cubed
- 1 carrot, sliced
- 1 cup dried black beans,
- sorted and rinsed
- 2 cups vegetable broth
- 2 teaspoons chili powder
- ½ teaspoon dried marjoram leaves
- ½ teaspoon salt
- ⅛ teaspoon freshly ground black pepper
- ⅛ teaspoon crushed red pepper flakes

1. In the Ninja Foodi PossibleCooker, combine all the ingredients.
2. Cover and cook on low for 7 to 8 hours, or until the beans and vegetables are tender, and serve.

Lentils with Vegetarian Hot Dogs

Prep time: 5 minutes | Cook time: 6 to 8 hours | Serves 8

- 2 cups barbecue sauce
- 3½ cups water
- 1 pound (454 g) dry lentils
- 1 package vegetarian hot dogs, sliced

1. Combine all ingredients in Ninja Foodi PossibleCooker. 2. Cover. Cook on low 6 to 8 hours.

"Famous" Baked Beans

Prep time: 20 minutes | Cook time: 3 to 6 hours | Serves 10

- 1 pound (454 g) ground beef
- ¼ cup minced onions
- 1 cup ketchup
- 4 (15-ounce / 425-g) cans pork and beans
- 1 cup brown sugar
- 2 tablespoons liquid smoke
- 1 tablespoon Worcestershire sauce

1. In a skillet over medium heat, brown the beef with the onions until fully cooked, then drain off any excess fat. Transfer the browned meat and onions to the Ninja Foodi PossibleCooker. 2. Add all remaining ingredients to the Ninja Foodi PossibleCooker, stirring well to ensure everything is combined. 3. Cover and cook on high for 3 hours, or set to low and cook for 5 to 6 hours, until flavors are fully developed and the dish is heated through.

Hearty Ninja Foodi PossibleCooker Vegetarian Chili

Prep time: 15 minutes | Cook time: 4 to 8 hours | Serves 4

- 1 (28-ounce / 794-g) can chopped whole tomatoes, with the juice
- 1 medium green bell pepper, chopped
- 1 (15-ounce / 425-g) can red beans, drained and rinsed
- 1 (15-ounce / 425-g) can black beans, drained and rinsed
- 1 yellow onion, chopped
- 1 tablespoon olive oil
- 1 tablespoon onion powder
- 1 teaspoon garlic powder
- 1 teaspoon cayenne pepper
- 1 teaspoon paprika
- ½ teaspoon sea salt
- ½ teaspoon black pepper
- 1 large Hass avocado, pitted, peeled, and chopped, for garnish

1. Combine the tomatoes, bell pepper, red beans, black beans, and onion in the Ninja Foodi PossibleCooker. Sprinkle with the onion powder, garlic powder, cayenne pepper, paprika, ½ teaspoon salt, and ½ teaspoon black pepper. 2. Cover and cook on high for 4 to 6 hours or on low for 8 hours, or until thick. 3. Season with salt and black pepper if needed. Served hot, garnished with some of the avocado.

White Beans with Kale

Prep time: 15 minutes | Cook time: 7½ hours | Serves 2

- 1 onion, chopped
- 1 leek, white part only, sliced
- 2 celery stalks, sliced
- 2 garlic cloves, minced
- 1 cup dried white lima beans or cannellini beans, sorted and rinsed
- 2 cups vegetable broth
- ½ teaspoon salt
- ½ teaspoon dried thyme leaves
- ⅛ teaspoon freshly ground black pepper
- 3 cups torn kale

1. In the Ninja Foodi PossibleCooker, add all ingredients except for the kale, stirring to combine evenly. 2. Cover and cook on low for about 7 hours, or until the beans are fully tender. 3. Once the beans are cooked, add the kale to the Ninja Foodi PossibleCooker and stir it into the mixture. 4. Cover again and switch to high, cooking for an additional 30 minutes or until the kale is tender but still has a bit of firmness. Serve warm.

Creamy White Beans

Prep time: 20 minutes | Cook time: 4 hours | Serves 6

- 2 cups dried small white beans, soaked overnight in water to cover and drained
- ½ cup extra-virgin olive oil
- 6 cloves garlic, sliced
- 1 tablespoon finely chopped
- fresh rosemary
- 6 to 8 cups chicken broth
- 1½ teaspoons salt
- ½ teaspoon freshly ground black pepper

1. Place the beans into the insert of a 5- to 7-quart Ninja Foodi PossibleCooker. In a small skillet, warm the oil over very low heat. Add the garlic and rosemary, letting them gently cook for about 10 minutes, ensuring the garlic stays light and doesn't brown. 2. Pour the infused oil, garlic, and rosemary into the Ninja Foodi PossibleCooker with the beans. Add 6 cups of chicken broth and stir to combine. Cover and cook on high for 3 hours, periodically checking that the beans aren't sticking; add more broth if needed. Cover and continue cooking for an additional hour, or until the beans are tender. Season with salt and pepper to taste. 3. Keep the Ninja Foodi PossibleCooker on the warm setting and serve the beans directly from it for easy serving.

Caribbean Black Beans

Prep time: 15 minutes | Cook time: 5 hours | Serves 8

- 1 pound (454 g) black turtle beans, soaked overnight in water to cover and drained
- 2 tablespoons olive oil
- 2 medium red onions, finely chopped
- 2 cloves garlic, minced
- 1 Anaheim chile, seeded and finely chopped
- 1 medium red bell pepper,
- seeded and finely chopped
- 1 teaspoon jerk seasoning
- 1 bay leaf
- 1 (14- to 15-ounce / 397- to 425-g) can crushed plum tomatoes, with their juice
- 2 tablespoons fresh lime juice
- 5 cups chicken broth

1. Place the beans in the insert of a 5- to 7-quart Ninja Foodi PossibleCooker. In a large skillet, heat the oil over medium-high heat. Add the onions, garlic, chile, bell pepper, jerk seasoning, and bay leaf, and sauté until the vegetables are softened and fragrant. 2. Add the tomatoes to the skillet and mix well, then transfer everything to the Ninja Foodi PossibleCooker. Stir in the lime juice and chicken broth to combine. 3. Cover the Ninja Foodi

PossibleCooker and set it to cook on high for 5 hours, checking the liquid level at the 3- and 4-hour marks. Stir and add additional broth if needed to ensure the beans stay moist. Cook until the beans are tender and creamy. 4. Keep the Ninja Foodi PossibleCooker on the warm setting to serve the beans directly from the cooker.

No-Meat Baked Navy Beans

Prep time: 10 minutes | Cook time: 6½ to 9½ hours | Serves 8 to 10

- 1 pound (454 g) dried navy beans
- 6 cups water
- 1 small onion, chopped
- ¾ cup ketchup
- ½ cup brown sugar
- ¾ cup water
- 1 teaspoon dry mustard
- 3 tablespoons dark molasses
- 1 teaspoon salt

1. Soak beans in water overnight in large soup kettle. Cook beans in water until soft, about 1½ hours. Drain, discarding bean water. 2. Stir together all ingredients in Ninja Foodi PossibleCooker. Mix well. 3. Cover. Cook on low 5 to 8 hours, or until beans are well flavored but not breaking down.

Mixed Ninja Foodi PossibleCooker Beans

Prep time: 10 minutes | Cook time: 4 to 5 hours | Serves 6

- 1 (16-ounce / 454-g) can kidney beans, drained
- 1 (15½-ounce / 439-g) can baked beans, undrained
- 1 pint home-frozen, or 1 (1-pound / 454-g) package frozen, lima beans
- 1 pint home-frozen, or 1 (1-pound / 454-g) package
- frozen, green beans
- 4 slices lean turkey bacon, browned and crumbled
- ½ cup ketchup
- ⅓ cup sugar
- ⅓ cup brown sugar
- 2 tablespoons vinegar
- ½ teaspoon salt

1. Place the beans and bacon in the Ninja Foodi PossibleCooker, stirring to combine evenly. 2. In a separate bowl, mix together all remaining ingredients until well blended, then pour this mixture over the beans and bacon. Stir thoroughly to ensure everything is well incorporated. 3. Cover the Ninja Foodi PossibleCooker and cook on low for 4 to 5 hours, allowing the flavors to meld together.

Chapter 3

Stews and Soups

Chapter 3 Stews and Soups

Split Pea Soup with Ham

Prep time: 15 minutes | Cook time: 4 hours | Serves 8

- 2½ quarts water
- 1 ham hock or pieces of cut-up ham
- 2½ cups split peas, dried
- 1 medium onion, chopped
- 3 medium carrots, cut in small pieces
- Salt and pepper to taste

1. Start by bringing water to a boil in a saucepan on the stovetop. 2. While the water heats, place all remaining ingredients into the Ninja Foodi PossibleCooker. Once the water is boiling, add it to the Ninja Foodi PossibleCooker and stir everything together until well combined. 3. Cover the Ninja Foodi PossibleCooker and cook on high for about 4 hours, or until the vegetables are tender to your liking. 4. If using a ham hock, remove it from the soup once cooked, debone it, and cut the meat into chunks. Stir the meat back into the soup before serving for added flavor.

Savory Beef Stock

Prep time: 20 minutes | Cook time: 4½ to 10½ hours | Makes about 6 cups

- ¼ cup tomato paste
- 2 teaspoons sugar
- 2 teaspoons salt
- 1 teaspoon freshly ground black pepper
- 4 cloves garlic, minced
- 2 teaspoons dried thyme
- 1 teaspoon dried sage
- 3 large sweet onions, coarsely chopped
- 4 large carrots, coarsely chopped
- 1½ pounds (680 g) beef stew meat, cut into 1-inch pieces
- 2 pounds (907 g) meaty beef bones, sawed in a few pieces (your butcher can do this for you)
- 4 cups water

1. Preheat the oven to 425ºF (220ºC). Line a baking sheet with a silicone baking liner or aluminum foil. 2. Stir together the tomato paste, sugar, salt, pepper, garlic, thyme, and sage in a large mixing bowl. Put the vegetables, meat, and bones in the bowl and rub the paste over them until they are coated. 3. Spread the mixture out on the baking sheet and bake for 30 minutes, turning the pieces once during the cooking process. Transfer the mixture with any liquid to the insert of a 5- to 7-quart Ninja Foodi PossibleCooker. Add the water and stir to blend. 4. Cover and cook on high for 4 to 5 hours or on low for 8 to 10 hours. Remove the solids from the stock, then strain the stock through a fine-mesh sieve into a bowl. Allow the stock to cool, and skim off the fat from the surface. 5. Refrigerate the stock for 3 days or freeze for up to 8 weeks. The meat from the stock may be frozen separately and used in soups, stews, or chilies.

South Indian Tomato and Pepper Soup

Prep time: 15 minutes | Cook time: 3 to 6 hours | Serves 6

- 6⅓ cups hot water
- ⅓ cup split yellow pigeon peas
- 1 tablespoon tamarind paste
- 1 heaped teaspoon black peppercorns
- 1 heaped teaspoon cumin seeds
- 1 teaspoon turmeric
- 20 curry leaves
- 6 tomatoes, roughly chopped
- 2 dried red chiles
- 4 garlic cloves, roughly chopped
- 4-inch piece fresh ginger, roughly chopped
- Handful coriander stalks, finely chopped
- Coriander leaves to garnish

1. Add all ingredients to the Ninja Foodi PossibleCooker, ensuring they are well combined. Cover and cook on low for 6 hours, or on high for 3 to 4 hours, until the ingredients are tender. 2. Once cooked, use an immersion blender directly in the Ninja Foodi PossibleCooker, or transfer the mixture to a regular blender, to purée until smooth. 3. Taste the soup and add additional salt, if needed, to enhance flavor. 4. Serve garnished with fresh coriander leaves for a burst of color and freshness.

Creamy Clam Chowder Delight

Prep time: 10 minutes | Cook time: 2 to 3 hours | Serves 3

- 1 (15-ounce / 425-g) can New England-style clam chowder
- 1½ cups milk or half-and-half
- 1 (6½-ounce / 184-g) can minced clams, undrained
- Half a stick (¼ cup) butter
- ¼ cup cooking sherry

1. Mix all ingredients together in Ninja Foodi PossibleCooker. 2. Heat on low for 2 to 3 hours, or until good and hot.

Taco Soup with Hominy

Prep time: 15 minutes | Cook time: 4 hours | Serves 8

- 1 pound (454 g) ground beef
- 1 envelope dry ranch dressing mix
- 1 envelope dry taco seasoning mix
- 3 (12-ounce / 340-g) cans Rotel tomatoes, undrained
- 2 (24-ounce / 680-g) cans
- pinto beans, undrained
- 1 (24-ounce / 680-g) can hominy, undrained
- 1 (14½-ounce / 411-g) can stewed tomatoes, undrained
- 1 onion, chopped
- 2 cups water

1. In a skillet over medium heat, brown the meat until evenly cooked, then transfer it to the Ninja Foodi PossibleCooker. 2. Add all remaining ingredients to the Ninja Foodi PossibleCooker and stir thoroughly to ensure everything is well mixed. 3. Cover and cook on low for 4 hours, allowing flavors to blend and the dish to heat through.

Hearty Bean Medley Soup

Prep time: 10 minutes | Cook time: 5½ to 13 hours | Serves 10 to 12

- 1 cup dry Great Northern beans
- 1 cup dry red beans or pinto beans
- 4 cups water
- 1 (28-ounce / 794-g) can diced tomatoes
- 1 medium onion, chopped
- 2 tablespoons vegetable bouillon granules, or 4 bouillon cubes
- 2 garlic cloves, minced
- 2 teaspoons Italian seasoning, crushed
- 1 (9-ounce / 255-g) package frozen green beans, thawed

1. Soak and rinse dried beans. 2. Combine all ingredients except

green beans in Ninja Foodi PossibleCooker. 3. Cover. Cook on high 5½ to 6½ hours, or on low 11 to 13 hours. 4. Stir green beans into soup during last 2 hours.

Indian Cauliflower-Potato Soup

Prep time: 20 minutes | Cook time: 8 hours | Serves 2

- 1 onion, chopped
- 2 garlic cloves, sliced
- 2 teaspoons grated fresh ginger
- 1 tablespoon green curry paste
- 2 Yukon Gold potatoes, peeled and cubed
- 2 cups cauliflower florets
- 3 cups vegetable broth
- 1 bay leaf
- ½ teaspoon salt
- ⅛ teaspoon freshly ground black pepper
- ½ cup light cream

1. Place all ingredients, except the light cream, into the Ninja Foodi PossibleCooker, stirring to combine. 2. Cover and cook on low for 8 hours, allowing the flavors to meld and ingredients to become tender. 3. After cooking, remove and discard the bay leaf. 4. Use an immersion blender or potato masher to blend or mash the soup until it has a slightly textured consistency, leaving a bit of chunkiness. 5. Stir in the light cream, then ladle the soup into bowls and serve warm.

Hearty Veggie-Beef Delight Soup

Prep time: 20 minutes | Cook time: 4 to 8 hours | Serves 6 to 8

- 1 pound (454 g) browned ground beef, or 2 cups stewing beef
- 2 cups sliced carrots
- 1 pound (454 g) frozen green beans, thawed
- 1 (14½-ounce / 411-g) can corn, drained, or 1 (16-ounce / 454-g) bag frozen corn, thawed
- 1 (28-ounce / 794-g) can
- diced tomatoes
- 3 cups beef or vegetable broth
- 3 teaspoons instant beef bouillon
- 2 teaspoons Worcestershire sauce
- 1 tablespoon sugar
- 1 tablespoon minced onion
- 1 (10¾-ounce / 305-g) can cream of celery soup

1. Place meat in bottom of Ninja Foodi PossibleCooker. 2. Add remaining ingredients except celery soup. Mix well. 3. Stir in soup. 4. Cover. Cook on low 7 to 8 hours, or on high 4 hours. 5. If using stewing meat, shred and mix through soup just before serving. 6. Serve.

Jambalaya Soup

Prep time: 15 minutes | Cook time: 6 to 7 hours | Serves 8

- 1 tablespoon extra-virgin olive oil
- 6 cups chicken broth
- 1 (28-ounce / 794-g) can diced tomatoes
- 1 pound (454 g) spicy organic sausage, sliced
- 1 cup chopped cooked chicken
- 1 red bell pepper, chopped
- ½ sweet onion, chopped
- 1 jalapeño pepper, chopped
- 2 teaspoons minced garlic
- 3 tablespoons Cajun seasoning
- ½ pound (227 g) medium shrimp, peeled, deveined, and chopped
- ½ cup sour cream, for garnish
- 1 avocado, diced, for garnish
- 2 tablespoons chopped cilantro, for garnish

1. Begin by lightly greasing the insert of the Ninja Foodi PossibleCooker with olive oil. 2. Add the broth, diced tomatoes, sausage, chicken, red bell pepper, onion, jalapeño, garlic, and Cajun seasoning to the Ninja Foodi PossibleCooker. Stir to combine all ingredients. 3. Cover and cook on low for 6 to 7 hours, allowing the flavors to meld and the ingredients to tenderize. 4. When there are 30 minutes left, stir in the shrimp and continue cooking on low until the shrimp are cooked through. 5. Serve the dish warm, topped with sour cream, diced avocado, and fresh cilantro for added flavor and texture.

Mexican Tomato-Corn Soup

Prep time: 10 minutes | Cook time: 6 to 8 hours | Serves 8

- 1 medium onion, diced
- 1 medium green bell pepper, diced
- 1 clove garlic, minced
- 1 cup diced carrots
- 1 (14½-ounce / 411-g) can low-sodium diced Italian tomatoes
- 2½ cups low-sodium tomato juice
- 1 quart low-fat, low-sodium chicken broth
- 3 cups corn, frozen or canned
- 1 (4-ounce / 113-g) can chopped chilies, undrained
- 1 teaspoon chili powder
- 1½ teaspoons ground cumin
- Dash cayenne powder

1. Place all ingredients into the Ninja Foodi PossibleCooker, stirring gently to combine. 2. Cover the Ninja Foodi PossibleCooker and set it to cook on low for 6 to 8 hours, until everything is tender and flavors are fully blended.

Chicken Rice and Veggies Soup

Prep time: 30 minutes | Cook time: 4 to 8 hours | Serves 8

- 4 cups chicken broth
- 4 cups cooked chicken, cubed or shredded
- 1⅓ cups cut-up celery
- 1⅓ cups diced carrots
- 1 quart water
- 1 cup long-grain rice, uncooked

1. Place all ingredients into the Ninja Foodi PossibleCooker, making sure to stir them gently to combine. 2. Cover and cook on low for 4 to 8 hours, or until the vegetables reach your preferred level of tenderness. Adjust seasoning if needed before serving.

Sweet and Spiced Lentil Delight

Prep time: 10 minutes | Cook time: 8 hours | Serves 2

- 1 cup dried lentils, rinsed and sorted
- 1 apple, cored, peeled, and diced
- 1 cup diced onion
- ¼ cup diced celery
- 1 teaspoon fresh thyme
- ¼ teaspoon ground cinnamon
- ¼ teaspoon ground allspice
- ⅛ teaspoon sea salt
- ¼ cup dry red wine
- 3 cups low-sodium chicken or vegetable broth

1. Put all the ingredients into the Ninja Foodi PossibleCooker and stir to combine. 2. Cover and cook on low for 6 to 8 hours, until the lentils are very soft.

Quick and Easy Chinese Chicken Vegetable Soup

Prep time: 5 minutes | Cook time: 1 to 2 hours | Serves 6

- 3 (14½-ounce / 411-g) cans chicken broth
- 1 (16-ounce / 454-g) package frozen stir-fry vegetable blend
- 2 cups cooked chicken, cubed
- 1 teaspoon minced fresh ginger root
- 1 teaspoon soy sauce

1. Mix all ingredients in Ninja Foodi PossibleCooker. 2. Cover and cook on high for 1 to 2 hours, depending upon how crunchy or soft you like your vegetables to be.

Veracruz-Inspired Seafood Soup

Prep time: 30 minutes | Cook time: 5 to 6 hours | Serves 8

- 4 (6-inch) corn tortillas, cut into thin strips
- 2 tablespoons vegetable oil
- 1 medium onion, finely chopped
- 2 cloves garlic, minced
- 1 jalapeño pepper, seeded and finely chopped
- 2 medium red bell peppers, finely chopped
- 1 teaspoon ground cumin
- 1 teaspoon dried oregano
- 1 (12-ounce / 340-g) bottle Corona or other light Mexican beer
- 1 (28- to 32-ounce / 794- to 907-g) can chopped tomatoes, with their juice
- 1 (8-ounce / 227-g) bottle clam juice
- 1 pound (454 g) sea bass, halibut, or red snapper fillets, cut into 1-inch chunks
- 2 cups cooked long-grain rice
- ½ cup finely chopped fresh cilantro
- Salt and freshly ground black pepper

1. Place the tortillas in the bottom of the insert of a 5- to 7-quart Ninja Foodi PossibleCooker. 2. Heat the oil in a large skillet over medium-high heat. Add the onion, garlic, jalapeño, bell peppers, cumin, and oregano and sauté until the vegetables are softened, about 5 minutes. 3. Deglaze the pan with the beer, scraping up any browned bits from the bottom of the skillet. Transfer the contents of the skillet to the slow-cooker insert and stir to combine with the tortillas. Stir in the tomatoes and clam juice. 4. Cover and cook on low for 4 to 5 hours. Stir in the fish, rice, and cilantro and cook for an additional 1 hour, until the fish is cooked through. 5. Season with salt and pepper before serving.

New Mexico-Style Beef and Sausage Stew

Prep time: 15 minutes | Cook time: 8½ to 10½ hours | Serves 8

- 2 pounds (907 g) stewing meat or steak, cubed, divided
- Salt to taste
- Pepper to taste
- 1 tablespoon oil
- 5 to 6 potatoes, cubed,
- divided
- 6 to 8 carrots, diced, divided
- 1 to 2 (4¼-ounce / 120-g) cans chopped green chilies, divided
- 1½ pounds (680 g) raw pork sausage, crumbled, divided

1. Salt and pepper stewing meat. Brown in oil in skillet. 2. Place half the stewing meat in bottom of Ninja Foodi PossibleCooker. 3.

Layer half the vegetables and chilies over the beef. Crumble half the sausage over top. Sprinkle each layer with salt and pepper. 4. Continue layering until all ingredients are used. 5. Cover. Cook on high until ingredients begin to boil. Then turn cooker to low for 8 to 10 hours. Do not lift lid and do not stir during cooking. 6. Serve.

Easy Potato Soup

Prep time: 10 minutes | Cook time: 5 hours | Serves 8

- 3 cups chicken broth
- 1 (2-pound / 907-g) bag frozen hash brown potatoes
- 1½ teaspoons salt
- ¾ teaspoon pepper
- 3 cups milk
- 3 cups shredded Monterey Jack or Cheddar cheese

1. Add the chicken broth, potatoes, salt, and pepper to the Ninja Foodi PossibleCooker, stirring to combine. 2. Cover and cook on high for about 4 hours, or until the potatoes are tender. 3. With the broth and potatoes still in the Ninja Foodi PossibleCooker, lightly mash the potatoes, leaving some larger chunks for texture. 4. Stir in the milk and cheese, mixing thoroughly until well blended. 5. Cover again and cook on high until the cheese has melted and the soup is hot and creamy. Serve warm and enjoy!

Smoky Polish Sausage and Northern Bean Soup

Prep time: 45 minutes | Cook time: 9½ hours | Serves 10

- 1 (1-pound / 454-g) package dried Great Northern beans
- 1 (28-ounce / 794-g) can whole tomatoes
- 2 (8-ounce / 227-g) cans tomato sauce
- 2 large onions, chopped
- 3 cloves garlic, minced
- 1 teaspoon salt
- ¼ to ½ teaspoon pepper, according to your taste preference
- 3 celery ribs, sliced
- Bell pepper, sliced
- Large ham bone or ham hock
- 1 to 2 pounds (454 to 907 g) smoked sausage links, sliced

1. Cover beans with water and soak for 8 hours. Rinse and drain. 2. Place beans in 6-qt. cooker and cover with water. 3. Combine all other ingredients, except sausage, in large bowl. Stir into beans in Ninja Foodi PossibleCooker. 4. Cover. Cook on high 1 to 1½ hours. Reduce to low. Cook 7 hours. 5. Remove ham bone or hock and debone. Stir ham pieces back into soup. 6. Add sausage links. 7. Cover. Cook on low 1 hour.

Southwest Corn Soup

- 2 (4-ounce / 113-g) cans chopped green chilies, undrained
- 2 small zucchini, cut into bite-sized pieces
- 1 medium onion, thinly sliced
- 3 cloves garlic, minced
- 1 teaspoon ground cumin
- 3 (14½-ounce / 411-g) cans fat-free, sodium-reduced

- chicken broth
- 1½ to 2 cups cooked turkey, shredded
- 1 (15-ounce / 425-g) can chickpeas or black beans, rinsed and drained
- 1 (10-ounce / 283-g) package frozen corn
- 1 teaspoon dried oregano
- ½ cup chopped cilantro

1. Add all ingredients to the Ninja Foodi PossibleCooker, stirring to combine evenly. 2. Cover and cook on low for 4 hours, until flavors are blended and the dish is thoroughly heated. Serve warm and enjoy!

Hearty Monterey Bay Bean Soup with Chiles and Tortilla Strips

- ⅓ cup vegetable oil
- 1 large onion, finely chopped
- 1 clove garlic, minced
- 4 Anaheim chiles, seeded and chopped
- 1½ teaspoons chili powder
- 1 (14- to 15-ounce / 397- to 425-g) can chopped tomatoes, drained
- 2 (14- to 15-ounce / 397- to 425-g) cans pinto beans, drained and rinsed
- 6 cups chicken broth
- 2 cups cooked chorizo

- sausage, crumbled (optional)
- Salt and freshly ground black pepper
- 2 cups broken fried tortilla strips
- ½ cup shredded mild Cheddar or Monterey Jack cheese
- ½ cup sour cream, for garnish
- 4 green onions, chopped, using the white and tender green parts, for garnish
- ½ cup finely minced fresh cilantro, for garnish

1. Heat the oil in a large skillet over medium heat. Add the onion, garlic, and chiles and sauté until the vegetables are softened, about 5 minutes. Stir in the chili powder and cook, stirring, for about 1 minute, until fragrant. 2. Transfer the contents of the skillet to the insert of a 5- to 7-quart Ninja Foodi PossibleCooker. Add the tomatoes, beans, broth, and sausage (if using). 3. Cover the Ninja Foodi PossibleCooker and cook the soup on high for 3 to 4 hours or on low for 7 to 8 hours. 4. Season with salt and pepper. Add the tortilla strips to the soup, cover, and let stand for 10 minutes, until the strips just begin to soften. 5. Divide the cheese among 8 bowls and ladle the soup over. 6. Garnish each serving with a dollop of sour cream, chopped green onion, and minced cilantro.

Hearty Vegetarian Chili Soup with Kale and Cannellini Beans

- 1 large onion, chopped
- 1 tablespoon margarine
- 1 clove garlic, finely chopped
- 2 teaspoons chili powder
- ½ teaspoon dried oregano, crumbled
- 2 (14½-ounce / 411-g) cans vegetable broth
- 1 (14½-ounce / 411-g) can

- no-salt-added stewed or diced tomatoes
- 5 cups water
- ½ teaspoon salt
- ¼ teaspoon black pepper
- ¾ pound (340 g) fresh kale
- ⅓ cup white long-grain rice
- 1 (19-ounce / 539-g) can cannellini beans, drained and rinsed

1. Sauté onion in skillet with margarine until tender. 2. Add garlic, chili powder, and oregano. Cook for 30 seconds. Pour into Ninja Foodi PossibleCooker. 3. Add remaining ingredients except kale, rice, and beans. 4. Cover. Cook on low 7 hours, or on high 3 to 4 hours. 5. Cut kale stalks into small pieces and chop leaves coarsely. 6. Add to soup with rice and beans. 7. Cover. Cook on high 1 to 2½ hours more, or until rice is tender and kale is done to your liking.

Bratwurst Stew

- 2 (10¾-ounce / 305-g) cans fat-free chicken broth
- 4 medium carrots, sliced
- 2 ribs of celery, cut in chunks
- 1 medium onion, chopped
- 1 teaspoon dried basil

- ½ teaspoon garlic powder
- 3 cups chopped cabbage
- 2 (1-pound / 454-g) cans Great Northern beans, drained
- 5 fully cooked bratwurst links, cut into ½-inch slices

1. Place all ingredients into the Ninja Foodi PossibleCooker, stirring to ensure they are evenly mixed. 2. Set the Ninja Foodi PossibleCooker to high and cook for 3 to 4 hours, or until the vegetables reach your desired tenderness. Adjust seasoning if needed before serving.

Kansas City Steak Soup

Prep time: 15 minutes | Cook time: 5 to 6 hours | Serves 6 to 8

- 2 pounds (907 g) sirloin, cut into ½-inch pieces
- 1½ teaspoons salt
- ½ teaspoon freshly ground black pepper
- 4 tablespoons (½ stick) unsalted butter
- 2 medium yellow onions, finely chopped
- 4 medium carrots, finely chopped
- 4 stalks celery with leaves, finely chopped
- 3 tablespoons all-purpose flour
- 6 cups beef broth
- 1 (16-ounce / 454-g) package frozen corn, defrosted
- 2 cups frozen petite peas, defrosted

1. Season the sirloin pieces evenly with salt and pepper. In a large skillet, heat 1 tablespoon of butter over medium-high heat. Add the sirloin a few pieces at a time, browning on all sides. Once browned, transfer the meat to the insert of a 5- to 7-quart Ninja Foodi PossibleCooker. 2. In the same skillet, melt the remaining 3 tablespoons of butter over medium-high heat. Add the onions, carrots, and celery, and sauté for about 5 minutes, or until the onions are fragrant and the vegetables start to soften. 3. Sprinkle the flour over the vegetables and cook for an additional 2 to 3 minutes, stirring continuously. Gradually add the broth, stirring until the mixture begins to boil and thicken. Pour this mixture into the Ninja Foodi PossibleCooker with the browned meat. 4. Cover and cook on low for 4 to 5 hours, or until the meat is tender. 5. Remove the cover, add the corn and peas, and stir to combine. Cover and cook for an additional 45 minutes to 1 hour, or until the vegetables are heated through. Serve warm.

Wild Rice and Lentil Soup

Prep time: 5 minutes | Cook time: 5 to 8 hours | Serves 8 to 10

- ½ cup dried lentils, sorted, rinsed, and drained
- 3 cups water
- 1 (6-ounce / 170-g) package long-grain and wild rice blend, with spice packet
- 1 (14-ounce / 397-g)
- vegetable broth
- 1 (10-ounce / 283-g) package frozen mixed vegetables
- 1 cup skim milk
- ½ cup reduced-fat mild Cheddar cheese, shredded

1. Place the lentils in a bowl and cover them with water. Let them soak overnight or for 6 to 8 hours, then drain and discard the soaking water. 2. Add the drained lentils and all other ingredients to the Ninja Foodi PossibleCooker, including 3 cups of fresh water. Stir everything together until well mixed. 3. Cover and cook on low for 5 to 8 hours, or until the vegetables reach your desired tenderness. Adjust seasoning as needed before serving.

Hearty Sauerkraut and Potato Soup with Polish Sausage

Prep time: 15 minutes | Cook time: 2 to 8 hours | Serves 8

- 1 pound (454 g) smoked Polish sausage, cut into ½-inch pieces
- 5 medium potatoes, cubed
- 2 large onions, chopped
- 2 large carrots, cut into ¼-inch slices
- 1 (42-ounce / 1.2-kg) can chicken broth
- 1 (32-ounce / 907-g) can or bag sauerkraut, rinsed and drained
- 1 (6-ounce / 170-g) can tomato paste

1. Combine all ingredients in large Ninja Foodi PossibleCooker. Stir to combine. 2. Cover. Cook on high 2 hours, and then on low 6 to 8 hours. 3. Serve.

Fajita Stew

Prep time: 15 minutes | Cook time: 6½ to 8½ hours | Serves 8

- 2½ pounds (1.1 kg) boneless beef top round steak
- 1 onion, chopped
- 1 (1-ounce / 28-g) envelope dry fajita seasoning mix (about 2 tablespoons)
- 1 (14-ounce / 397-g) diced tomatoes, undrained
- 1 red bell pepper, cut into 1-inch pieces
- ¼ cup flour
- ¼ cup water

1. Trim any excess fat from the beef and cut it into 2-inch pieces. Place the beef and onion in the Ninja Foodi PossibleCooker, stirring to combine. 2. In a bowl, mix the fajita seasoning with the undrained tomatoes, then pour this mixture over the beef in the Ninja Foodi PossibleCooker. 3. Layer the cut-up peppers on top of the beef and tomato mixture. 4. Cover and cook on low for 6 to 8 hours, or until the beef is tender. 5. In a small bowl, combine the flour and water, stirring until smooth. 6. Gradually pour the flour mixture into the Ninja Foodi PossibleCooker, stirring well to combine. 7. Cover and cook on high for an additional 15 to 20 minutes, stirring occasionally, until the sauce has thickened. Serve warm.

Creamy Tomato Soup

Prep time: 20 minutes | Cook time: 1½ hours | Serves 6

- 1 (26-ounce / 737-g) can condensed tomato soup, plus 6 ounces (170 g) water to equal 1 quart
- ½ teaspoon salt (optional)
- Half a stick butter
- 8 tablespoons flour
- 1 quart milk (whole or reduced-fat)

1. In the Ninja Foodi PossibleCooker, add the tomato soup, a pinch of salt if desired, and butter. Stir well until everything is combined. 2. Cover the Ninja Foodi PossibleCooker and cook on high for 1 hour. 3. While the soup heats, combine the flour and 1 cup of milk in a 2-quart microwave-safe container. Whisk until there are no large lumps, then gradually whisk in the remaining milk until only small lumps remain. 4. Microwave the flour-milk mixture on high for 3 minutes, then remove and stir until smooth. Return to the microwave and cook for an additional 3 minutes on high, stirring again to ensure a smooth consistency. 5. Slowly pour the thickened milk mixture into the hot tomato soup in the Ninja Foodi PossibleCooker, stirring to incorporate. 6. Allow the soup to heat thoroughly for another 10 to 15 minutes, then serve warm.

Vietnamese Beef and Noodle Soup

Prep time: 15 minutes | Cook time: 8 hours | Serves 2

- ½ pound (227 g) chuck eye roast, cut into 1-inch pieces
- 1 onion, chopped
- 3 radishes, sliced
- 3 garlic cloves, minced
- 1 serrano chile, minced
- 1 tablespoon grated fresh ginger
- 1 tablespoon freshly squeezed lime juice
- 2 teaspoons fish sauce
- 1 star anise pod
- 3 cups beef stock
- ½ teaspoon dried basil leaves
- ½ teaspoon dried marjoram leaves
- ½ teaspoon salt
- ¼ teaspoon freshly ground black pepper
- ½ (12 ounces / 340 g) package udon noodles or spaghetti
- 1 tablespoon minced fresh basil leaves
- 1 tablespoon minced fresh mint

1. Place the beef, onion, radishes, garlic, chile, ginger, lime juice, fish sauce, star anise, stock, basil, marjoram, salt, and pepper in the Ninja Foodi PossibleCooker. Stir to ensure everything is well mixed. 2. Cover the Ninja Foodi PossibleCooker and cook on low for 7½ hours, allowing the flavors to meld and the beef to become tender. 3. After 7½ hours, add the udon noodles, stirring them into the soup. Increase the heat to high, cover, and cook for an additional 20 minutes, or until the noodles are soft. 4. Just before serving, stir in the fresh basil and mint. Ladle the soup into bowls and serve immediately for the best flavor.

Creamy Green Chili Corn Chowder

Prep time: 15 minutes | Cook time: 7¼ to 8¼ hours | Serves 8

- 1 (16-ounce / 454-g) can cream-style corn
- 3 potatoes, peeled and diced
- 2 tablespoons chopped fresh chives
- 1 (4-ounce / 113-g) can diced green chilies, drained
- 1 (2-ounce / 57-g) jar chopped pimentos, drained
- ½ to ¾ cup chopped cooked ham
- 2 (10½-ounce / 298-g) cans chicken broth
- Salt to taste
- Pepper to taste
- Tabasco sauce to taste
- 1 cup milk
- Shredded Monterey Jack cheese

1. Combine all ingredients except milk and cheese in Ninja Foodi PossibleCooker. 2. Cover. Cook on low 7 to 8 hours or until potatoes are tender. 3. Stir in milk. Heat until hot. 4. Top individual servings with cheese. Serve.

Hearty Toscano Sausage and Potato Soup

Prep time: 20 minutes | Cook time: 6 to 8 hours | Serves 4 to 6

- 2 medium russet potatoes
- 1 pound (454 g) spicy Italian sausage
- 5½ cups chicken stock or low-sodium chicken broth
- 2 cups chopped kale
- ½ teaspoon crushed red pepper flakes (optional)
- ½ cup cream or evaporated milk

1. Cut potatoes into ½-inch cubes. Place in Ninja Foodi PossibleCooker. 2. Grill, broil, or brown sausage in a nonstick skillet. When cool enough to handle, cut into ½-inch-thick slices. 3. Add sliced sausage to Ninja Foodi PossibleCooker. Stir in all remaining ingredients, except cream. 4. Cover and cook on low 6 to 8 hours. 5. Fifteen to 20 minutes before serving, add cream or evaporated milk and cook until soup is heated through.

Garbanzo Souper

- 1 pound (454 g) dry garbanzo beans
- 4 ounces (113 g) raw baby carrots, cut in halves
- 1 large onion, diced
- 3 ribs celery, cut in 1-inch pieces
- 1 large green pepper, diced
- ½ teaspoon dried basil
- ½ teaspoon dried oregano
- ½ teaspoon dried rosemary
- ½ teaspoon dried thyme
- 2 (28-ounce / 794-g) cans vegetable broth
- 1 broth can of water
- 1 (8-ounce / 227-g) can tomato sauce
- 8 ounces (227 g) prepared hummus
- ½ teaspoon sea salt

1. Soak the beans overnight, then drain and place them at the bottom of the Ninja Foodi PossibleCooker. 2. Add the carrots, onion, celery, and green pepper on top of the beans. 3. Sprinkle the mixture with basil, oregano, rosemary, and thyme to season. 4. Pour the broth and water over the ingredients to cover them. 5. Cover the Ninja Foodi PossibleCooker and cook on high for 6 hours, allowing the beans to become tender. 6. About 30 minutes before serving, stir in the tomato sauce, hummus, and salt. Continue cooking until everything is heated through. 7. Serve warm and enjoy.

Hearty Kale and Cannellini Stew with Farro

- 4 cups vegetable or chicken stock
- 1 (14-ounce / 397-g) can diced fire-roasted tomatoes
- 1 cup farro, rinsed
- 1 large yellow onion, chopped
- 2 medium carrots, halved lengthwise and thinly sliced crosswise
- 2 stalks celery, coarsely chopped
- 4 cloves garlic, minced
- ½ teaspoon red pepper flakes
- ¼ teaspoon sea salt
- 4 cups fresh kale, stemmed and coarsely chopped
- 1 (15-ounce / 425-g) can cannellini beans, rinsed and drained
- 3 tablespoons fresh lemon juice
- ½ cup crumbled feta cheese
- Fresh flat-leaf parsley or basil, chopped, for garnish

1. Combine the stock, tomatoes, farro, onion, carrots, celery, and garlic in the Ninja Foodi PossibleCooker. 2. Add the red pepper flakes and ¼ teaspoon salt. 3. Cover and cook on high for 2 hours, or until the farro is tender yet chewy. 4. Add the kale, cannellini,

and lemon juice and stir. Cover and cook 1 additional hour. 5. Serve hot, sprinkled with the feta cheese and parsley.

Corn Chowder

- 6 slices bacon, diced
- ½ cup chopped onions
- 2 cups diced peeled potatoes
- 2 (10-ounce / 283-g) packages frozen corn
- 1 (16-ounce / 454-g) can cream-style corn
- 1 tablespoon sugar
- 1 teaspoon Worcestershire sauce
- 1 teaspoon seasoned salt
- ¼ teaspoon pepper
- 1 cup water

1. In a skillet, cook the bacon over medium heat until it is crisp. Remove the bacon and set aside, reserving the drippings in the skillet. 2. Add the onions and potatoes to the skillet with the bacon drippings and sauté for about 5 minutes. Drain any excess grease. 3. Transfer the bacon, sautéed onions, potatoes, and all other ingredients to the Ninja Foodi PossibleCooker. Stir everything together until well mixed. 4. Cover and cook on low for 6 to 7 hours, until the flavors are well combined and the dish is fully cooked. Serve warm.

Hearty Beef and Black Bean Soup

- 1 pound (454 g) extra-lean ground beef
- 2 (14½-ounce / 411-g) cans fat-free, low-sodium chicken broth
- 1 (14½-ounce / 411-g) can low-sodium, diced tomatoes, undrained
- 8 green onions, thinly sliced
- 3 medium carrots, thinly sliced
- 2 celery ribs, thinly sliced
- 2 garlic cloves, minced
- 1 tablespoon sugar
- 1½ teaspoons dried basil
- ½ teaspoon salt
- ½ teaspoon dried oregano
- ½ teaspoon ground cumin
- ½ teaspoon chili powder
- 2 (15-ounce / 425-g) cans black beans, rinsed and drained
- 1½ cups rice, cooked

1. In a nonstick skillet over medium heat, cook beef until no longer pink. Drain. 2. Place beef in Ninja Foodi PossibleCooker. 3. Add remaining ingredients except black beans and rice. 4. Cover. Cook on high 1 hour. 5. Reduce to low. Cook 4 to 5 hours, or until vegetables are tender. 6. Add beans and rice. 7. Cook 1 hour longer on low, or until heated through.

Savory Homemade Sausage and Kale Soup

Prep time: 15 minutes | Cook time: 6 hours | Serves 6

- 3 tablespoons olive oil, divided
- 1½ pounds (680 g) sausage, without casing
- 6 cups chicken broth
- 2 celery stalks, chopped
- 1 carrot, diced
- 1 leek, thoroughly cleaned and chopped
- 2 teaspoons minced garlic
- 2 cups chopped kale
- 1 tablespoon chopped fresh parsley, for garnish

1. Lightly grease the insert of the Ninja Foodi PossibleCooker with 1 tablespoon of the olive oil. 2. In a large skillet over medium-high heat, heat the remaining 2 tablespoons of the olive oil. Add the sausage and sauté until it is cooked through, about 7 minutes. 3. Transfer the sausage to the insert, and stir in the broth, celery, carrot, leek, and garlic. 4. Cover and cook on low for 6 hours. 5. Stir in the kale. 6. Serve topped with the parsley.

Steak and Black Bean Chili Delight

Prep time: 15 minutes | Cook time: 7½ hours | Serves 2

- 1 pound (454 g) sirloin tip steak, cubed
- 1 onion, chopped
- 2 garlic cloves, minced
- 1 jalapeño pepper, minced
- 1 chipotle chili in adobo sauce, minced
- 2 tablespoons adobo sauce
- 1 (15 ounces / 425 g) can black beans, rinsed and drained
- 1 (15 ounces / 425 g) can diced tomatoes with green chiles
- 1 (8 ounces / 227 g) can tomato sauce
- 1 teaspoons chili powder
- ½ teaspoon dried oregano
- ½ teaspoon salt
- ⅛ teaspoon freshly ground black pepper
- ⅛ teaspoon ground cayenne pepper
- 1 tablespoon cornstarch
- ¼ cup water

1. In the Ninja Foodi PossibleCooker, combine all the ingredients except the cornstarch and water, and stir. 2. Cover and cook on low for 7 hours. 3. In a small bowl, stir together the cornstarch and water. Stir the mixture into the Ninja Foodi PossibleCooker. 4. Cover and cook on high for 20 to 30 minutes, or until thickened, and serve.

Chicken Vegetable Soup

Prep time: 10 minutes | Cook time: 6 to 8 hours | Serves 6

- 1 cup frozen corn
- 2 ribs celery, chopped
- 1 (6-ounce / 170-g) can tomato paste
- ¼ cup dry lentils, rinsed
- 1 tablespoon sugar
- 1 tablespoon Worcestershire sauce
- 2 teaspoons dried parsley flakes
- 1 teaspoon dried marjoram
- 2 cups cooked chicken breast, cubed

1. Add all ingredients to the Ninja Foodi PossibleCooker, except for the chicken, and stir to combine. 2. Cover and cook on low for 6 to 8 hours, allowing the flavors to blend. 3. One hour before the end of the cooking time, stir in the chicken, ensuring it's well incorporated. Continue cooking until the full time is reached and the chicken is heated through. Serve warm.

Chapter
4

Beef, Pork, and Lamb

Chapter 4 Beef, Pork, and Lamb

Beef and Lentil Medley

Prep time: 35 minutes | Cook time: 6 to 8 hours | Serves 12

- 1 medium onion
- 3 whole cloves
- 5 cups water
- 1 pound (454 g) lentils
- 1 teaspoon salt
- 1 bay leaf
- 1 pound (454 g) (or less) ground beef, browned and
- drained
- ½ cup ketchup
- ¼ cup molasses
- 2 tablespoons brown sugar
- 1 teaspoon dry mustard
- ¼ teaspoon Worcestershire sauce
- 1 onion, finely chopped

1. Stick cloves into whole onion. Set aside. 2. In large saucepan, combine water, lentils, salt, bay leaf, and whole onion with cloves. Simmer 30 minutes. 3. Meanwhile, combine all remaining ingredients in Ninja Foodi PossibleCooker. Stir in simmered ingredients from saucepan. Add additional water if mixture seems dry. 4. Cover. Cook on low 6 to 8 hours (check to see if lentils are tender).

Lemon Pork

Prep time: 15 minutes | Cook time: 7 to 8 hours | Serves 6

- 3 tablespoons extra-virgin olive oil, divided
- 1 tablespoon butter
- 2 pounds (907 g) pork loin roast
- ½ teaspoon salt
- ¼ teaspoon freshly ground
- black pepper
- ¼ cup chicken broth
- Juice and zest of 1 lemon
- 1 tablespoon minced garlic
- ½ cup heavy (whipping) cream

1. Lightly grease the insert of the Ninja Foodi PossibleCooker with 1 tablespoon of olive oil. 2. In a large skillet over medium-high heat, combine the remaining 2 tablespoons of olive oil and the butter, allowing it to melt. 3. Season the pork roast lightly with salt and pepper. Add the pork to the skillet and sear it on all sides until browned, about 10 minutes. Once browned, transfer the pork to the Ninja Foodi PossibleCooker insert. 4. In a small bowl, mix together the broth, lemon juice, lemon zest, and garlic until well combined. 5. Pour this broth mixture over the pork in the Ninja Foodi PossibleCooker. 6. Cover and cook on low for 7 to 8 hours, allowing the flavors to meld. 7. Before serving, stir in the heavy cream to create a rich sauce. Serve warm.

Corned Beef and Cabbage Medley

Prep time: 15 minutes | Cook time: 5 to 10 hours | Serves 12

- 3 large carrots, cut into chunks
- 1 cup chopped celery
- 1 teaspoon salt
- ½ teaspoon black pepper
- 1 cup water
- 1 (4-pound / 1.8-kg) corned
- beef
- 1 large onion, cut into pieces
- 4 potatoes, peeled and chunked
- Half a small head of cabbage, cut in wedges

1. Place carrots, celery, seasonings, and water in Ninja Foodi PossibleCooker. 2. Add beef. Cover with onions. 3. Cover. Cook on low 8 to 10 hours, or on high 5 to 6 hours. (If your schedule allows, this dish has especially good taste and texture if you begin it on high for 1 hour, and then turn it to low for 5 to 6 hours, before going on to Step 4.) 4. Lift corned beef out of cooker and add potatoes, pushing them to bottom of Ninja Foodi PossibleCooker. Return beef to cooker. 5. Cover. Cook on low 1 hour. 6. Lift corned beef out of cooker and add cabbage, pushing the wedges down into the broth. Return beef to cooker. 7. Cover. Cook on low 1 more hour. 8. Remove corned beef. Cool and slice on the diagonal. Serve surrounded by vegetables.

Creamy Scalloped Potatoes and Ham

Prep time: 20 minutes | Cook time: 4 to 5 hours | Serves 6

- 6 cups sliced, raw potatoes
- Salt and pepper to taste
- 1 (10¾-ounce / 305-g) can cream of mushroom or
- celery soup
- 1½ cups milk
- 1 pound (454 g) cooked ham, cubed

1. Layer the potatoes in the Ninja Foodi PossibleCooker, sprinkling each layer with salt and pepper for seasoning. 2. In a separate bowl, mix together the soup, milk, and ham until well combined. Pour this mixture evenly over the potatoes in the Ninja Foodi PossibleCooker. 3. Cover and cook on high for 3½ hours. Check for tenderness, and if needed, continue cooking for an additional ½ to 1½ hours until the potatoes are fully tender. Serve warm.

Swiss Steak

Prep time: 30 minutes | Cook time: 7 hours | Serves 4

- 1 (1-pound / 454-g) round steak, ¾ to 1-inch thick, cubed
- 1 (16-ounce / 454-g) can stewed tomatoes
- 3 carrots, halved lengthwise
- 2 potatoes, quartered
- 1 medium onion, quartered
- Garlic powder to taste (optional)

1. Layer all ingredients in your Ninja Foodi PossibleCooker in the order they are listed to ensure even cooking. 2. Cover the Ninja Foodi PossibleCooker and set it to low, cooking for about 7 hours, or until the meat and vegetables are tender but still moist and flavorful. Adjust seasoning if needed before serving.

Sweet Cola-Glazed Beef

Prep time: 5 minutes | Cook time: 8 to 10 hours | Serves 12

1 (2- to 3-pound / 907-g to 1.4-kg) chuck roast, cubed
1 package dry onion soup mix
1 (12-ounce / 340-g) can cola

1. Place meat in Ninja Foodi PossibleCooker. 2. Sprinkle soup mix over meat. Pour cola over all. 3. Cover. Cook on low 8 to 10 hours. 4. Serve.

Creamy Mushroom Meatballs with Noodles

Prep time: 7 minutes | Cook time: 4 to 5 hours | Serves 10 to 12

- 2 (10¾-ounce / 305-g) cans cream of mushroom soup
- 2 (8-ounce / 227-g) packages cream cheese, softened
- 1 (4-ounce / 113-g)
- can sliced mushrooms, undrained
- 1 cup milk
- 2 to 3 pounds (907 g to 1.4 kg) frozen meatballs

1. Combine soup, cream cheese, mushrooms, and milk in Ninja Foodi PossibleCooker. 2. Add meatballs. Stir. 3. Cover. Cook on low 4 to 5 hours. 4. Serve over noodles.

Veal Stew with Forty Cloves of Garlic

Prep time: 20 minutes | Cook time: 6 to 7 hours | Serves 6

- ½ cup all-purpose flour
- 1½ teaspoons salt
- ½ teaspoon freshly ground black pepper
- 2½ pounds (1.1 kg) boneless veal shoulder or shank, cut into 1-inch pieces
- 3 tablespoons extra-virgin olive oil
- ¼ cup tomato paste
- 1 teaspoon dried thyme
- ½ cup dry white wine or vermouth
- 1 cup chicken broth
- ½ cup beef broth
- 1 bay leaf
- 40 cloves garlic, peeled

1. In a large zipper-top plastic bag, combine the flour, salt, and pepper. Add the veal, seal the bag, and toss to coat the meat evenly, shaking off any excess flour. Heat the oil in a large skillet over high heat and, working in batches, add the veal pieces, browning them on all sides. 2. Transfer the browned veal to the insert of a 5- to 7-quart Ninja Foodi PossibleCooker. Once all the veal is browned, add the tomato paste, thyme, and white wine to the skillet. Scrape up any browned bits from the bottom of the pan, then add both broths and stir to combine. 3. Pour the contents of the skillet over the veal in the Ninja Foodi PossibleCooker. Add the bay leaf and garlic cloves, stirring to ensure everything is well distributed. Cover and cook on low for 6 to 7 hours, or until the veal is tender. 4. Use a slotted spoon to remove the veal from the Ninja Foodi PossibleCooker. Mash the softened garlic cloves into the sauce, then taste and adjust the seasoning if needed. Return the veal to the Ninja Foodi PossibleCooker, stir gently, and serve the stew warm.

Savory Barbecued Spoonburgers

Prep time: 15 minutes | Cook time: 3 to 8 hours | Serves 6 to 8

- 2 tablespoons oil
- 1½ pounds (680 g) ground beef
- ½ cup chopped onions
- ½ cup diced celery
- Half a green pepper, chopped
- 1 tablespoon Worcestershire sauce
- ½ cup ketchup
- 1 garlic clove, minced
- 1 teaspoon salt
- ¾ cup water
- ⅛ teaspoon pepper
- ½ teaspoon paprika
- 1 (6-ounce / 170-g) can tomato paste
- 2 tablespoons vinegar
- 2 teaspoons brown sugar
- 1 teaspoon dry mustard

1. Brown beef in oil in saucepan. Drain. 2. Combine all ingredients in Ninja Foodi PossibleCooker. 3. Cover. Cook on low 6 to 8 hours, or on high 3 to 4 hours. 4. Serve.

Sweet and Sour Tomato Meatballs

Prep time: 45 minutes | Cook time: 6 hours | Serves 6 to 8

Meatballs:

- 2 pounds (907 g) ground beef
- 1¼ cups bread crumbs
- 1½ teaspoons salt
- 1 teaspoon pepper
- 2 to 3 tablespoons Worcestershire sauce
- 1 egg
- ½ teaspoon garlic salt
- ¼ cup finely chopped onions

Sauce:

- 1 can pineapple chunks, juice reserved
- 3 tablespoons cornstarch
- ¼ cup cold water
- 1 to 1¼ cups ketchup
- ¼ cup Worcestershire sauce
- ¼ teaspoon salt
- ¼ teaspoon pepper
- ¼ teaspoon garlic salt
- ½ cup chopped green peppers

1. In a large bowl, combine all ingredients for the meatballs and mix well. Shape the mixture into 15 to 20 meatballs. In a skillet over medium heat, brown the meatballs, turning them to brown on all sides. Once browned, transfer the meatballs to the Ninja Foodi PossibleCooker. 2. Pour the juice from the canned pineapples into the skillet, stirring to incorporate it with any browned bits. 3. In a small bowl, mix the cornstarch with cold water until smooth, then add this mixture to the skillet. Stir until the sauce begins to thicken. 4. Add ketchup, Worcestershire sauce, salt, pepper, and garlic salt to the skillet, stirring to combine. Add in the green peppers and pineapple chunks, then pour the entire mixture over the meatballs in the Ninja Foodi PossibleCooker. 5. Cover the Ninja Foodi PossibleCooker and cook on low for 6 hours, allowing the flavors to meld. Serve warm.

Stuffed Cabbage

Prep time: 25 minutes | Cook time: 8 to 10 hours | Serves 8

- 4 cups water
- 12 large cabbage leaves, cut from head at base and washed
- 1 pound (454 g) lean ground beef or lamb
- ½ cup rice, cooked
- ½ teaspoon salt
- ¼ teaspoon black pepper
- ¼ teaspoon dried thyme
- ¼ teaspoon nutmeg
- ¼ teaspoon cinnamon
- 1 (6-ounce / 170-g) can tomato paste
- ¾ cup water

1. In a saucepan, bring 4 cups of water to a boil. Turn off the heat and place the cabbage leaves in the hot water to soak for 5 minutes. Remove the leaves, drain them well, and set aside to cool. 2. In a bowl, combine the ground beef, rice, salt, pepper, thyme, nutmeg, and cinnamon, mixing until evenly blended. 3. Take each cabbage leaf and place 2 tablespoons of the meat mixture in the center. Roll each leaf firmly around the filling, then stack the stuffed cabbage rolls in the Ninja Foodi PossibleCooker. 4. In a separate bowl, mix together the tomato paste and ¾ cup water until smooth. 5. Pour the tomato mixture over the cabbage rolls. Cover the Ninja Foodi PossibleCooker and cook on low for 8 to 10 hours, until the cabbage and filling are tender. Serve warm.

Spicy Shredded Beef Machaca

Prep time: 5 minutes | Cook time: 10 to 12 hours | Serves 12

- 1 (1½-pound / 680-g) lean beef roast
- 1 large onion, sliced
- 1 (4-ounce / 113-g) can chopped green chilies
- 2 low-sodium beef bouillon cubes
- 1½ teaspoons dry mustard
- ½ teaspoon garlic powder
- ¾ teaspoon seasoned salt
- ½ teaspoon black pepper
- 1 cup low-sodium salsa

1. Combine all ingredients except salsa in Ninja Foodi PossibleCooker. Add just enough water to cover. 2. Cover cooker and cook on low 10 to 12 hours, or until beef is tender. Drain and reserve liquid. 3. Shred beef using two forks to pull it apart. 4. Combine beef, salsa, and enough of the reserved liquid to make a desired consistency. 5. Serve.

Tomato Mexican Pot Roast

Prep time: 5 minutes | Cook time: 8 to 10 hours | Serves 8

- 1½ cups chunky salsa
- 1 (6-ounce / 170-g) can tomato paste
- 1 envelope dry taco seasoning mix
- 1 cup water
- 1 (3-pound / 1.4-kg) beef chuck roast
- ½ cup chopped cilantro

1. In a mixing bowl, combine the first four ingredients, stirring until well blended. 2. Place the roast in the Ninja Foodi PossibleCooker and pour the salsa mixture over the top, ensuring the meat is evenly coated. 3. Cover and cook on low for 8 to 10 hours, or until the beef is tender but still moist. Once done, transfer the roast to a serving platter. 4. Stir fresh cilantro into the sauce, then serve it alongside the beef for added flavor.

Indian-Spiced Brisket Delight

Prep time: 15 minutes | Cook time: 6 to 8 hours | Serves 6 to 8

- 2 tablespoons rapeseed oil
- 1 large onion, cut into rings
- 2 fresh red chiles, finely chopped
- 5 garlic cloves, puréed
- 1 tablespoon freshly grated ginger
- 1 tablespoon garam masala
- 2 teaspoons turmeric
- 1 tablespoon ground cumin
- 1 tablespoon coriander seeds, ground
- 4 to 6 chopped tomatoes
- 1 cup hot water
- 2 pounds (907 g) beef brisket
- 1 bunch fresh coriander leaves, chopped
- 2 fresh red chiles sliced
- 4 scallions, sliced

1. Heat the Ninja Foodi PossibleCooker to high or sauté, and add the oil. Stir in the onions and cook until they soften. Then add the chile, garlic, and ginger, and stir. 2. Add the garam masala, turmeric, cumin seeds, coriander seeds, and tomatoes, and mix. Then pour in the water and add the beef brisket. 3. Cover and cook on low for 8 hours, or on high for 6 hours, until the meat is tender. Remove the meat from the pan and cover it with foil to keep warm. 4. Using an immersion or regular blender, purée the juices and either simmer them on high, uncovered in the Ninja Foodi PossibleCooker, or transfer to the stovetop to produce a glaze (about 5 minutes). 5. Pull the meat apart with two forks and place on a platter. Pour the glaze over the meat and mix through. Garnish with fresh coriander leaves, sliced chiles, and scallions.

Spanish-Style Olive Meatloaf

Prep time: 20 minutes | Cook time: 7 hours | Serves 2

- 1 tablespoon butter
- 1 onion, finely chopped
- 2 garlic cloves, minced
- 1 egg
- ⅓ cup soft bread crumbs
- ½ teaspoon sweet paprika
- ½ teaspoon dried marjoram
- leaves
- ¼ teaspoon salt
- ¼ cup chopped green olives
- 1 pound (454 g) extra-lean ground beef
- ⅓ cup tomato sauce
- 1 tablespoon Dijon mustard

1. In a small skillet over medium heat, melt the butter. Add the onion and garlic, and sauté, stirring, until tender, about 6 minutes. Remove to a large bowl to cool for 15 minutes. 2. Add the egg, bread crumbs, paprika, marjoram, salt, and olives to the onion mixture and mix well. 3. Add the ground beef to the onion mixture and mix gently but thoroughly, using your hands. 4. Tear off 2 (18-inch-long) strips of heavy-duty aluminum foil. Fold each in half lengthwise twice. Place the foil pieces in the bottom of the Ninja Foodi PossibleCooker in an "X." 5. Form the meat mixture into a loaf and place it in the middle of the aluminum foil. 6. In a small bowl, mix the tomato sauce and mustard. Spoon the mixture over the loaf. 7. Cover and cook on low for 6 to 7 hours, or until the meatloaf registers 165ºF (74ºC) on a meat thermometer. 8. Using the foil strips as a sling, remove the meatloaf from the Ninja Foodi PossibleCooker to a platter. Cover with foil and let stand for 5 minutes. 9. Slice and serve.

A Hearty Western Casserole

Prep time: 10 minutes | Cook time: 1 hour | Serves 5

- 1 pound (454 g) ground beef, browned
- 1 (16-ounce / 454-g) can whole corn, drained
- 1 (16-ounce / 454-g) can red kidney beans, drained
- 1 (10¾-ounce / 305-g) can
- condensed tomato soup
- 1 cup Colby cheese
- ¼ cup milk
- 1 teaspoon minced dry onion flakes
- ½ teaspoon chili powder

1. In the Ninja Foodi PossibleCooker, combine the beef, corn, beans, soup, cheese, milk, chopped onion, and chili powder, stirring everything together until well mixed. 2. Cover and cook on low for 1 hour, allowing the flavors to meld and the cheese to melt. Serve warm.

Kielbasa and Cabbage

Prep time: 15 minutes | Cook time: 7 to 8 hours | Serves 6

- 1 (1½-pound / 680-g) head green cabbage, shredded
- 2 medium onions, chopped
- 3 medium red potatoes, peeled and cubed
- 1 red bell pepper, chopped
- 2 garlic cloves, minced
- ⅔ cup dry white wine
- 1½ pounds (680 g) Polish kielbasa, cut into 3-inch long links
- 1 (28-ounce / 794-g) can cut-up tomatoes with juice
- 1 tablespoon Dijon mustard
- ¾ teaspoon caraway seeds
- ½ teaspoon pepper
- ¾ teaspoon salt

1. Add all ingredients to the Ninja Foodi PossibleCooker, ensuring they are evenly mixed. 2. Cover the Ninja Foodi PossibleCooker and cook on low for 7 to 8 hours, or until the cabbage is tender and flavors have melded together. Serve warm for the best taste.

Sweet and Spicy Pork Chops

Prep time: 5 minutes | Cook time: 6 to 8 hours | Serves 4

- 4 frozen pork chops
- 1 cup Italian salad dressing
- ½ cup brown sugar
- ⅓ cup prepared spicy mustard

1. Place pork chops in Ninja Foodi PossibleCooker. 2. Mix remaining 3 ingredients together in a bowl. Pour over chops. 3. Cover and cook on low 6 to 8 hours, or until meat is tender but not dry.

Thaw the Roast Beef

Prep time: 20 minutes | Cook time: 7 to 9 hours | Serves 10

- 1 (3- to 4-pound / 1.4- to 1.8-kg) frozen beef roast
- 1½ teaspoons salt
- Pepper to taste
- 1 large onion
- ¼ cup flour
- ¾ cup cold water

1. Begin by placing the frozen roast directly into the Ninja Foodi PossibleCooker. Sprinkle with 1½ teaspoons of salt and a dash of pepper to season. Arrange sliced onions evenly over the top of the roast. 2. Cover the Ninja Foodi PossibleCooker and set it to high, cooking for 1 hour to jump-start the process. After the hour, switch the setting to low and continue cooking for an additional 6 to 8 hours, or until the meat becomes tender but remains juicy. 3. When the roast is nearly done, ladle out about 1¼ cups of the broth from the Ninja Foodi PossibleCooker into a small saucepan and bring it to a gentle boil over medium heat. 4. In a separate bowl, whisk the flour with cold water until there are no lumps. 5. Slowly add this flour mixture into the boiling broth, stirring constantly until it thickens into a smooth gravy. 6. Slice the roast and return it to the Ninja Foodi PossibleCooker along with the onions. Pour the gravy over the roast, keeping it on low to stay warm until serving.

Cheesy Mushroom Delight Meatballs

Prep time: 10 minutes | Cook time: 6 to 8 hours | Serves 12 to 15

- 1 (3- to 4-pound / 1.4- to 1.8-kg) bag prepared meatballs
- 3 (10¾-ounce / 305-g) cans cream of mushroom or cream of celery, soup
- 1 (4-ounce / 113-g) can button mushrooms
- 1 (16-ounce / 454-g) jar Cheese Whiz
- 1 medium onion, diced

1. Combine all ingredients in Ninja Foodi PossibleCooker. 2. Cover. Cook on low 6 to 8 hours. 3. Serve.

Give-Me-More Meatballs

Prep time: 30 minutes | Cook time: 6 to 10 hours | Serves 10

- 1½ cups chili sauce
- 1 cup grape or apple jelly
- 3 teaspoons brown spicy mustard
- 1 pound (454 g) ground beef
- 1 egg
- 3 tablespoons dry bread crumbs
- ½ teaspoon salt

1. In the Ninja Foodi PossibleCooker, combine the chili sauce, jelly, and mustard, stirring until well mixed. 2. Cover the Ninja Foodi PossibleCooker and set to high while preparing the meatballs. 3. In a mixing bowl, combine the remaining ingredients for the meatballs and mix thoroughly. Shape the mixture into 30 meatballs and arrange them on a baking pan. Bake at 400ºF (205ºC) for 15 to 20 minutes, until cooked through. Drain any excess fat. 4. Transfer the baked meatballs to the Ninja Foodi PossibleCooker, gently stirring to coat them evenly in the sauce. 5. Cover and cook on low for 6 to 10 hours, allowing the flavors to blend. Serve warm.

Italian Beef au Jus

Prep time: 10 minutes | Cook time: 8 hours | Serves 8

- 1 (3- to 5-pound / 1.4- to 2.3-kg) boneless beef roast
- 1 (10-ounce / 283-g) package dry au jus mix
- 1 package dry Italian salad dressing mix
- 1 (14½-ounce / 411-g) can beef broth
- Half a soup can water

1. Place the beef roast directly into the Ninja Foodi PossibleCooker. 2. In a separate bowl, mix together all remaining ingredients until well combined, then pour the mixture evenly over the roast, coating it thoroughly. 3. Cover the Ninja Foodi PossibleCooker and cook on low for 8 hours, allowing the flavors to infuse and the beef to become tender. 4. Before serving, slice the roast and serve with the flavorful juices from the Ninja Foodi PossibleCooker.

Garlic & Wine Pot Roast

Prep time: 10 minutes | Cook time: 6 to 7 hours | Serves 6 to 8

- 1 (4- to 5-pound / 1.8- to 2.3-kg) beef chuck roast
- 1 garlic clove, cut in half
- Salt to taste
- Pepper to taste
- 1 carrot, chopped
- 1 rib celery, chopped
- 1 small onion, sliced
- ¾ cup sour cream
- 3 tablespoons flour
- ½ cup dry white wine

1. Rub roast with garlic. Season with salt and pepper. Place in Ninja Foodi PossibleCooker. 2. Add carrots, celery, and onion. 3. Combine sour cream, flour, and wine. Pour into Ninja Foodi PossibleCooker. 4. Cover. Cook on low 6 to 7 hours.

Creamy Rice-Stuffed Meatballs

Prep time: 20 minutes | Cook time: 5 hours | Serves 5

- ¾ pound (340 g) extra-lean ground beef or ground turkey
- 1 cup skim milk
- ½ cup long-grain rice, uncooked
- 1 medium onion, chopped
- 1 cup dry bread crumbs
- ½ teaspoon salt
- Dash of black pepper
- 1 (10¾-ounce / 305-g) can low-fat, low-sodium cream of mushroom soup
- ½ cup skim milk

1. Combine meat, 1 cup skim milk, rice, onion, bread crumbs, salt, and pepper in a bowl. 2. Shape with an ice cream scoop. Place in Ninja Foodi PossibleCooker. 3. Mix together soup and ½ cup milk. Pour over meatballs. 4. Cover. Cook on low 5 hours. 5. Serve.

Pork Chops and Stuffing with Curry

Prep time: 10 minutes | Cook time: 6 to 7 hours | Serves 3 to 4

- 1 box stuffing mix
- 1 cup water
- 1 (10¾-ounce / 305-g) can cream of mushroom soup
- 1 teaspoon, or more, curry powder, according to your taste preference
- 3 to 4 pork chops

1. In a bowl, combine the stuffing mix with water until moistened. Place half of the stuffing mixture in an even layer at the bottom of the Ninja Foodi PossibleCooker. 2. In a separate bowl, mix the soup with the curry powder until well combined. Pour half of this soup mixture over the stuffing layer in the Ninja Foodi PossibleCooker. Place the pork chops on top of the soup layer. 3. Spread the remaining stuffing mixture over the pork chops, then pour the rest of the soup mixture on top, covering evenly. 4. Cover the Ninja Foodi PossibleCooker and cook on low for 6 to 7 hours, or until the pork is tender and fully cooked. 5. Serve warm, and enjoy the layered flavors.

Speedy Beef Chili

Prep time: 20 minutes | Cook time: 4 to 5 hours | Serves 4

- 1 pound (454 g) ground beef
- 1 onion, chopped
- 1 (16-ounce / 454-g) can stewed tomatoes
- 1 (11½-ounce / 326-g) can Hot V-8 juice

For Garnish:
- Sour cream
- Chopped green onions
- 2 (15-ounce / 425-g) cans pinto beans
- ¼ teaspoon cayenne pepper
- ½ teaspoon salt
- 1 tablespoon chili powder
- Shredded cheese
- Sliced ripe olives

1. Crumble ground beef in microwave-safe casserole. Add onion. Microwave, covered, on high 15 minutes. Drain. Break meat into pieces. 2. Combine all ingredients except garnish ingredients in Ninja Foodi PossibleCooker. 3. Cook on low 4 to 5 hours. 4. Garnish with sour cream, chopped green onions, shredded cheese, and sliced ripe olives.

Barbecued Beef Patties

Prep time: 20 minutes | Cook time: 3 to 6 hours | Makes 4 sandwiches

- 1 pound (454 g) ground beef
- ¼ cup chopped onions
- 3 tablespoons ketchup
- 1 teaspoon salt
- 1 egg, beaten
- ¼ cup seasoned bread crumbs
- 1 (18-ounce / 510-g) bottle of your favorite barbecue sauce

1. Combine beef, onions, ketchup, salt, egg, and bread crumbs. Form into 4 patties. Brown both sides lightly in skillet. Place in Ninja Foodi PossibleCooker. 2. Cover with barbecue sauce. 3. Cover. Cook on high 3 hours, or on low 6 hours.

Hearty Beef Chili

Prep time: 15 minutes | Cook time: 4 to 5 hours | Serves 6

- 1 pound (454 g) extra-lean ground beef
- 2 cloves garlic, chopped finely
- 2 tablespoons chili powder
- 1 teaspoon ground cumin
- 1 (28-ounce / 794-g) can crushed tomatoes
- 1 (15-ounce / 425-g) can red kidney beans, rinsed and drained
- 1 onion, chopped
- 1 (4-ounce / 113-g) can diced chilies, undrained
- 2 tablespoons tomato paste
- Fresh oregano sprigs for garnish

1. In a large nonstick skillet, brown beef and garlic over medium heat. Stir to break up meat. Add chili powder and cumin. Stir to combine. 2. Mix together tomatoes, beans, onion, chilies, and tomato paste in Ninja Foodi PossibleCooker. Add beef mixture and mix thoroughly. 3. Cook on high 4 to 5 hours, or until flavors are well blended. 4. Garnish with oregano to serve.

Harvest Kielbasa

Prep time: 20 minutes | Cook time: 4 to 8 hours | Serves 6

- 2 pounds (907 g) smoked kielbasa
- 3 cups unsweetened
- applesauce
- ½ cup brown sugar
- 3 medium onions, sliced

1. Slice the kielbasa into ¼-inch rounds and brown them in a skillet over medium heat. Drain any excess fat and set aside. 2. In a small bowl, mix together the applesauce and brown sugar until well combined. 3. In the Ninja Foodi PossibleCooker, layer the browned kielbasa slices, followed by the sliced onions, and top with the applesauce mixture. 4. Cover the Ninja Foodi PossibleCooker and cook on low for 4 to 8 hours, allowing the flavors to meld and the onions to soften. Serve warm.

Creamy Ham and Potato Bake

Prep time: 20 minutes | Cook time: 6 hours | Serves 6 to 8

- 5 medium Yukon gold or red potatoes, scrubbed and cut into ¼-inch-thick slices
- 1 medium onion, cut into half rounds
- 4 tablespoons (½ stick) unsalted butter, melted
- 1½ teaspoons salt
- 1 teaspoon freshly ground black pepper
- 2 cups leftover ham, cut into matchsticks (about 8 slices)
- 2 cups heavy cream
- 1 cup whole milk
- 1 tablespoon Dijon mustard
- 2 cups finely shredded Gruyère cheese
- ½ cup grated Parmigiano-Reggiano cheese

1. Sauté the sausages in a large skillet until browned on all sides. Transfer the sausages to the insert of a 5- to 7-quart Ninja Foodi PossibleCooker. 2. Mix the pineapple juice, cornstarch, and curry powder in a mixing bowl, and pour into the slow-cooker insert. Add the pineapple, cover, and cook on low for 4 to 5 hours, until the sausages are cooked through and the sauce is thickened. 3. Serve from the cooker set on warm.

Salsa-Infused Beef Brisket with Sweet and Baking Potatoes

Prep time: 20 minutes | Cook time: 2 to 10 hours | Serves 8

- 1 pound (454 g) baking potatoes, peeled and cut into 1-inch cubes
- 1 pound (454 g) sweet potatoes, peeled and cut into 1-inch cubes
- 1 (3- to 3½-pound / 1.4- to 1.6-kg) beef brisket, fat trimmed
- 1¼ cups salsa
- 2 tablespoons flour, or quick-cooking tapioca

1. Place both kinds of potatoes in the Ninja Foodi PossibleCooker. 2. Top with the brisket. 3. Put salsa and flour in a small bowl and mix well. Pour evenly over the meat. 4. Cover and cook on low 6½ to 10 hours, or on high 2 to 5½ hours, or until the meat is tender but not dry. 5. To serve, remove the meat from the cooker, keep warm, and allow to rest for 10 minutes. Then slice the meat across the grain. Place slices on a platter and top with the potatoes and sauce.

Chili

- 3 pounds (1.4 kg) beef stewing meat, browned
- 2 cloves garlic, minced
- ¼ teaspoon pepper
- ½ teaspoon cumin
- ¼ teaspoon dry mustard
- 1 (7½-ounce / 213-g) can jalapeño relish
- 1 cup beef broth
- 1 to 1½ onions, chopped, according to your taste preference
- ½ teaspoon salt
- ½ teaspoon dried oregano
- 1 tablespoon chili powder
- 1 (7-ounce / 198-g) can green chilies, chopped
- 1 (14½-ounce / 411-g) can stewed tomatoes, chopped
- 1 (15-ounce / 425-g) can tomato sauce
- 2 (15-ounce / 425-g) cans red kidney beans, rinsed and drained
- 2 (15-ounce / 425-g) cans pinto beans, rinsed and drained

1. Add all ingredients, except for the kidney and pinto beans, to the Ninja Foodi PossibleCooker, stirring to combine. 2. Cover and cook on low for 10 to 12 hours, or on high for 6 to 7 hours. Add the kidney and pinto beans halfway through the cooking time, stirring them in gently. 3. Once fully cooked, serve warm.

Pork Chops with Sage and Balsamic Vinegar

- ¼ cup olive oil
- 1 teaspoon salt
- ½ teaspoon freshly ground black pepper
- 6 (1-inch-thick) pork loin chops
- 12 dried figs, cut in half
- 2 medium onions, cut into half rounds
- 2 teaspoons finely chopped fresh sage leaves
- ½ cup balsamic vinegar
- ¼ cup chicken broth
- 2 tablespoons unsalted butter

1. In a large skillet, heat the oil over high heat. Season the pork chops with salt and pepper, then add them to the skillet. Brown the pork chops on all sides, then transfer them to a 5- to 7-quart Ninja Foodi PossibleCooker. Scatter the figs over the pork chops in the Ninja Foodi PossibleCooker. 2. In the same skillet, add the onions and sage, sautéing for about 5 minutes or until the onions soften. Pour in the vinegar to deglaze, scraping up any browned bits from the pan. Pour in the broth, stirring to combine, and then transfer everything from the skillet to the Ninja Foodi PossibleCooker over the pork chops and figs. 3. Cover the Ninja Foodi PossibleCooker and cook on high for 3½ to 4 hours, or on low for 6 to 8 hours, until the pork is tender. Carefully remove the pork chops and cover with foil to keep warm. 4. Use an immersion blender to purée the sauce directly in the Ninja Foodi PossibleCooker, then whisk in the butter until the sauce is smooth. Return the pork to the Ninja Foodi PossibleCooker, set to warm, and serve with the rich fig and onion sauce.

Creamy Scalloped Potatoes with Ham

- 2 to 3 pounds (907 g to 1.4 kg) potatoes, peeled, sliced, divided
- 1 (12-ounce / 340-g) package, or 1 pound (454 g), cooked ham, cubed, divided
- 1 small onion, chopped, divided
- 2 cups shredded Cheddar cheese, divided
- 1 (10¾-ounce / 305-g) can cream of celery or mushroom soup
- Nonstick cooking spray

1. Spray the interior of the cooker with nonstick cooking spray. 2. Layer ⅓ each of the potatoes, ham, onion, and cheese into the cooker. 3. Repeat twice. 4. Spread soup on top. 5. Cover and cook on low 6 to 8 hours, or until potatoes are tender.

Beef Risotto

Prep time: 20 minutes | Cook time: 5 hours | Serves 2

- ½ pound (227 g) lean ground beef
- 1½ cups Arborio rice
- 1 onion, chopped
- 2 garlic cloves, minced
- ¼ cup dry white wine

- 4 cups beef stock
- ½ teaspoon salt
- ⅛ teaspoon freshly ground black pepper
- ½ cup grated Parmesan cheese
- 1 tablespoon butter

1. In a medium skillet over medium heat, cook the ground beef, stirring occasionally to break up the meat, until browned, about 10 minutes. Add the rice to the skillet and cook for another 2 to 3 minutes, stirring continuously to toast the rice lightly. Drain any excess fat. 2. Transfer the beef and rice mixture to the Ninja Foodi PossibleCooker. Add the chopped onion and garlic, then pour in the wine and stock. Season with salt and pepper, and stir to combine all ingredients evenly. 3. Cover the Ninja Foodi PossibleCooker and cook on low for 5 hours, allowing the flavors to meld. 4. Just before serving, stir in the cheese and butter, then let the mixture sit for about 5 minutes to melt and enrich the flavor. Serve warm and enjoy.

Chinese-Style Pork Chops

Prep time: 10 minutes | Cook time: 4 hours | Serves 6

- 6 (1-inch-thick) blade, shoulder, or sirloin pork chops
- 1 medium onion, sliced
- 2 garlic cloves, minced
- ½ cup soy sauce
- 1½ teaspoons Chinese black vinegar or white vinegar

- ¼ cup packed brown sugar
- ½ teaspoon ground ginger
- ¼ teaspoon Chinese five-spice powder
- 2 cups snap peas

1. Arrange the pork chops in the Ninja Foodi PossibleCooker, piercing them with a fork to help the flavors absorb. Scatter the onion slices over the pork. In a small bowl, mix together the garlic, soy sauce, vinegar, brown sugar, ginger, and five-spice powder until well blended, then pour the mixture over the pork chops. Cover and cook on low for 4 hours, letting the pork infuse with the marinade. 2. About 20 minutes before serving, add the snap peas to the Ninja Foodi PossibleCooker. Cover and cook until the snap peas are crisp-tender. Serve warm with a side of rice.

Chapter
5

Poultry

Chapter 5 Poultry

Tuscan Herb Chicken

Prep time: 25 minutes | Cook time: 6 hours | Serves 4

- 2 (14½-ounce / 411-g) cans Italian stewed tomatoes, undrained
- 10 small red potatoes (about 1 pound / 454 g), quartered
- 1 medium onion, chopped
- 1 (6-ounce / 170-g) can tomato paste
- 2 fresh rosemary sprigs
- 4 garlic cloves, minced
- 1 teaspoon olive oil
- ½ teaspoon dried basil
- 1 teaspoon Italian seasoning, divided
- 1 (3- to 4-pound / 1.4- to 1.8-kg) broiler/fryer chicken, cut up and skin removed
- ½ teaspoon salt
- ½ teaspoon pepper
- 1 (5¾-ounce / 163-g) jar pimiento-stuffed olives, drained

1. In a 5-quart Ninja Foodi PossibleCooker, combine the first eight ingredients. Stir in ½ teaspoon Italian seasoning. Place chicken on top. Sprinkle with salt, pepper and remaining Italian seasoning. Top with olives. 2. Cover and cook on low for 6 to 7 hours or until chicken is tender. Discard rosemary sprigs before serving.

Barbecued Chicken Breasts

Prep time: 10 minutes | Cook time: 3 to 8 hours | Serves 8

- 8 boneless, skinless chicken breast halves
- 1 (8-ounce / 227-g) can low-sodium tomato sauce
- 1 (8-ounce / 227-g) can water
- 2 tablespoons brown sugar
- 2 tablespoons prepared mustard
- 2 tablespoons
- Worcestershire sauce
- ¼ cup cider vinegar
- ½ teaspoon salt
- ¼ teaspoon black pepper
- Dash of garlic powder
- Dash of dried oregano
- 3 tablespoons onion, chopped
- Nonfat cooking spray

1. Arrange the chicken pieces in a single layer, or as close to it as possible, in a Ninja Foodi PossibleCooker that's been sprayed with nonfat cooking spray to prevent sticking. 2. In a separate bowl, mix together all remaining ingredients until well combined, then pour the mixture evenly over the chicken in the Ninja Foodi PossibleCooker. 3. Cover and cook on low for 6 to 8 hours, or on high for 3 to 4 hours, until the chicken is tender. 4. For a thicker sauce, remove the lid during the last hour of cooking to allow some liquid to evaporate. Serve warm.

Chicken Mushroom Farro Risotto

Prep time: 15 minutes | Cook time: 4 to 7 hours | Serves 4

- 2¼ cups chicken stock
- 1 cup whole farro
- 1 pound (454 g) cremini or button mushrooms, halved, or quartered if large
- 2 leeks, white and light green parts only, halved, sliced, and rinsed
- 1 bay leaf
- ¼ teaspoon ground nutmeg
- 1¼ teaspoons sea salt
- ¼ teaspoon black pepper
- 4 small boneless, skinless chicken thighs (about 1 pound / 454 g)
- 1 (3-inch) piece Parmesan cheese rind
- ⅓ cup grated Parmesan, plus more for serving (optional)
- 2 tablespoons unsalted butter, cut into pieces, for serving (optional)
- ¼ cup chopped fresh flat-leaf parsley, for serving (optional)

1. In the Ninja Foodi PossibleCooker, combine the stock, farro, mushrooms, leeks, and Parmesan rind. Season with 1¼ teaspoons salt, ¼ teaspoon pepper, a bay leaf, and a pinch of nutmeg. Stir to mix the ingredients well. 2. Place the chicken pieces on top of the other ingredients in the Ninja Foodi PossibleCooker. Cover and cook on low for 6 to 7 hours or on high for 4 to 5 hours, until the chicken is tender and the farro is cooked. 3. Before serving, remove and discard the Parmesan rind and bay leaf. Shred the chicken into large pieces and stir it back into the risotto mixture. Add the grated Parmesan and stir until melted, and stir in the butter for extra richness, if desired. 4. Garnish with fresh parsley and additional grated Parmesan for serving, if desired, and enjoy the risotto warm.

Savory Wild Rice Chicken Casserole

Prep time: 15 minutes | Cook time: 4 to 6 hours | Serves 8 to 10

- 2 cups wild rice, uncooked
- ½ cup slivered almonds
- ½ cup chopped onions
- ½ cup chopped celery
- 8 to 12 ounces (227 to 340 g) can mushrooms, drained
- 2 cups cooked, cut-up chicken
- 6 cups chicken broth
- ¼-½ teaspoon salt
- ¼ teaspoon pepper
- ¼ teaspoon garlic powder
- 1 tablespoon chopped parsley

1. Wash and drain rice. 2. Combine all ingredients in Ninja Foodi PossibleCooker. Mix well. 3. Cover. Cook on low 4 to 6 hours, or until rice is finished. Do not remove lid before rice has cooked 4 hours.

Spicy Chicken Curry

Prep time: 25 minutes | Cook time: 6 to 8 hours | Serves 8

- 4 pounds (1.8 kg) chicken pieces, with bones
- Water
- 2 onions, diced
- 1 (10-ounce / 283-g) package frozen chopped spinach, thawed and squeezed dry
- 1 cup plain yogurt
- 2 to 3 diced red potatoes
- 3 teaspoons salt
- 1 teaspoon garlic powder
- 1 teaspoon ground ginger
- 1 teaspoon ground cumin
- 1 teaspoon ground coriander
- 1 teaspoon pepper
- 1 teaspoon ground cloves
- 1 teaspoon ground cardamom
- 1 teaspoon ground cinnamon
- ½ teaspoon chili powder
- 1 teaspoon red pepper flakes
- 3 teaspoons turmeric

1. Place the chicken in a large Ninja Foodi PossibleCooker and cover it with water. 2. Cover the Ninja Foodi PossibleCooker with a lid and cook on high for 2 hours, or until the chicken is tender and cooked through. 3. Once cooked, drain the chicken and remove it from the Ninja Foodi PossibleCooker. Allow it to cool for a few moments, then cut or shred it into small pieces. Return the shredded chicken to the Ninja Foodi PossibleCooker. 4. Add the remaining ingredients to the Ninja Foodi PossibleCooker, mixing well to combine. 5. Cover the Ninja Foodi PossibleCooker again and cook on low for 4 to 6 hours, or until the potatoes are tender. 6. Serve warm and enjoy!

Chicken, Corn, and Stuffing

Prep time: 5 minutes | Cook time: 2 to 2½ hours | Serves 4

- 4 boneless, skinless chicken breast halves
- 1 (6-ounce / 170-g) box stuffing mix for chicken
- 1 (16-ounce / 454-g)
- package frozen whole-kernel corn
- Half a stick butter, melted
- 2 cups water

1. Arrange the chicken pieces at the bottom of the Ninja Foodi PossibleCooker. 2. In a mixing bowl, combine all remaining ingredients thoroughly. Spoon this mixture evenly over the chicken in the Ninja Foodi PossibleCooker. 3. Cover the Ninja Foodi PossibleCooker and set it to cook on high for 2 to 2½ hours, or until the chicken is tender and the stuffing has absorbed the flavors and dried slightly. Serve warm and enjoy!

Spicy Buffalo Chicken Cream Sauce

Prep time: 10 minutes | Cook time: 7½ hours | Serves 2

- 1 onion, chopped
- 3 garlic cloves, minced
- 1 cup sliced cremini mushrooms
- 3 celery stalks, sliced
- 1 red bell pepper, sliced
- 2 tablespoons minced celery leaves
- 5 boneless, skinless chicken thighs, cubed
- 3 tablespoons all-purpose flour
- ½ teaspoon dried marjoram
- leaves
- ½ teaspoon salt
- ⅛ teaspoon freshly ground black pepper
- 1¼ cups chicken stock
- ¼ cup Buffalo wing hot sauce
- 1 bay leaf
- 3 ounces (85 g) cream cheese, cubed
- ¼ cup sour cream
- ¼ cup crumbled blue cheese

1. In the Ninja Foodi PossibleCooker, combine the onion, garlic, mushrooms, celery, bell pepper, and celery leaves. 2. In a large bowl, toss the chicken thighs with the flour, marjoram, salt, and pepper, and place them on top of the vegetables in the Ninja Foodi PossibleCooker. 3. In a small bowl, mix the stock with the hot sauce and bay leaf; pour the mixture into the Ninja Foodi PossibleCooker. 4. Cover and cook on low for 7 hours, and then remove and discard the bay leaf. 5. Stir in the cream cheese and sour cream, cover, and cook on low for 20 to 30 minutes more, or until the cream cheese is melted. Gently stir. 6. Stir in the blue cheese and serve.

Tangy Sweet and Sour Chicken Delight

Prep time: 20 minutes | Cook time: 6 to 8 hours | Serves 4

- Cooking spray or 1 tablespoon extra-virgin olive oil
- 1 medium onion, chopped
- 2 tablespoons minced garlic (about 6 cloves)
- 1 green bell pepper, seeded and roughly chopped
- 1 red bell pepper, seeded and roughly chopped
- 1 pound (454 g) boneless, skinless chicken thighs, cut into ½-inch cubes
- ¼ cup or low-sodium chicken stock
- 3 tablespoons packed brown sugar
- 3 tablespoons rice vinegar
- ½ teaspoon kosher salt, plus more for seasoning
- ½ teaspoon ground white pepper, plus more for seasoning
- 1 (8-ounce / 227-g) can pineapple chunks, drained
- 4 teaspoons cornstarch, mixed with 4 teaspoons water

1. Use the cooking spray or olive oil to coat the inside (bottom and sides) of the Ninja Foodi PossibleCooker. Add the onion, garlic, bell peppers, chicken, chicken stock, brown sugar, vinegar, salt, and pepper. Stir to combine. Cover and cook on low for 6 to 8 hours. 2. About 30 minutes before serving, stir together the pineapple and cornstarch in a medium bowl until well combined. Add the mixture to the Ninja Foodi PossibleCooker, stir to combine, cover, and continue cooking until the sauce begins to thicken. 3. Season with additional salt and pepper, as needed.

Curried Chicken Divan

Prep time: 15 minutes | Cook time: 3 hours | Serves 6

- 4 tablespoons (½ stick) unsalted butter
- 1½ teaspoons curry powder
- ¼ cup all-purpose flour
- 2 cups chicken broth
- 1 cup evaporated milk
- 8 chicken breast halves, skin and bones removed
- 1½ cups finely shredded sharp Cheddar cheese

1. In a saucepan over medium-high heat, melt the butter. Once melted, add the curry powder and sauté for about 30 seconds to release its flavor. 2. Stir in the flour and continue to cook for 3 minutes, whisking constantly to avoid lumps. Gradually add the broth, bringing the mixture to a boil. Once boiling, incorporate the milk, then remove the sauce from heat and allow it to cool slightly. 3. In the insert of a 5- to 7-quart Ninja Foodi PossibleCooker, place the chicken, arranging it evenly. Pour the cooled sauce over the chicken, ensuring it's well covered. 4. Cover the Ninja Foodi PossibleCooker and cook on high for 3 hours, allowing the chicken to absorb the flavors. 5. After 3 hours, sprinkle the cheese over the chicken, cover again, and cook for an additional hour, or until the chicken is thoroughly cooked and tender. 6. Serve the chicken warm straight from the Ninja Foodi PossibleCooker, enjoying the rich and flavorful dish.

Zesty Cranberry-Orange Glazed Turkey Breast

Prep time: 10 minutes | Cook time: 3½ to 8 hours | Serves 9

- ½ cup orange marmalade
- 1 (16-ounce / 454-g) can whole cranberries in sauce
- 2 teaspoons orange zest, grated
- 1 (3-pound / 1.4-kg) turkey breast

1. Combine marmalade, cranberries, and zest in a bowl. 2. Place the turkey breast in the Ninja Foodi PossibleCooker and pour half the orange-cranberry mixture over the turkey. 3. Cover. Cook on low 7 to 8 hours, or on high 3½ to 4 hours, until turkey juices run clear. 4. Add remaining half of orange-cranberry mixture for the last half hour of cooking. 5. Remove turkey to warm platter and allow to rest for 15 minutes before slicing. 6. Serve with orange-cranberry sauce.

Chili Barbecued Chicken Wings

Prep time: 5 minutes | Cook time: 2 to 8 hours | Serves 10

- 5 pounds (2.3 kg) chicken wings, tips cut off
- 1 (12-ounce / 340-g) bottle chili sauce
- ⅓ cup lemon juice
- 1 tablespoon Worcestershire sauce
- 2 tablespoons molasses
- 1 teaspoon salt
- 2 teaspoons chili powder
- ¼ teaspoon hot pepper sauce
- Dash garlic powder

1. Place the chicken wings in the Ninja Foodi PossibleCooker, arranging them evenly. 2. In a separate bowl, mix together all remaining ingredients until well combined, then pour this mixture over the wings in the Ninja Foodi PossibleCooker. 3. Cover the Ninja Foodi PossibleCooker with the lid and cook on low for 6 to 8 hours, or on high for 2 to 3 hours, until the wings are tender and infused with flavor. Serve hot and enjoy!

Southern Barbecue Turkey Spaghetti Sauce

Prep time: 20 minutes | Cook time: 4 to 5 hours | Serves 12

- 1 pound (454 g) lean ground turkey
- 2 medium onions, chopped
- 1½ cups sliced fresh mushrooms
- 1 medium green bell pepper, chopped
- 2 garlic cloves, minced
- 1 (14½-ounce / 411-g) can diced tomatoes, undrained
- 1 (12-ounce / 340-g) can tomato paste
- 1 (8-ounce / 227-g) can tomato sauce
- 1 cup ketchup
- ½ cup fat-free beef broth
- 2 tablespoons Worcestershire sauce
- 2 tablespoons brown sugar
- 1 tablespoon ground cumin
- 2 teaspoons chili powder
- 12 cups spaghetti, cooked

1. In a large nonstick skillet, cook the turkey, onions, mushrooms, green pepper, and garlic over medium heat until meat is no longer pink. Drain. 2. Transfer to Ninja Foodi PossibleCooker. Stir in tomatoes, tomato paste, tomato sauce, ketchup, broth, Worcestershire sauce, brown sugar, cumin, and chili powder. Mix well. 3. Cook on low 4 to 5 hours. Serve over spaghetti.

Hainanese Chicken

Prep time: 30 minutes | Cook time: 4 hours | Serves 6

Chicken and Broth:

- 2 bunches whole scallions, trimmed
- 1 bunch cilantro
- 1 whole chicken (about 4 pounds / 1.8 kg)
- 4 fresh or dried Asian chiles
- 4 whole star anise
- 8 (¼-inch) slices peeled

Rice:

- 1 garlic clove, minced
- 1½ teaspoons finely grated peeled fresh ginger

fresh ginger
- 2 garlic cloves
- 2 teaspoon peppercorns, preferably white
- 8 cups boiling water
- ½ cup low-sodium soy sauce
- 2 tablespoons fish sauce

- 1½ cups jasmine rice
- Hot chili oil, for serving

1. Begin by preheating your 5- to 6-quart Ninja Foodi PossibleCooker. For the chicken and broth, place the chopped scallions (reserving 2 for garnish) and half of the cilantro in the bottom of the Ninja Foodi PossibleCooker. Lay the chicken on top, then arrange the chiles, star anise, ginger, garlic, and peppercorns around the chicken. 2. Pour in the boiling water, soy sauce, and fish sauce. Note that the liquid may not completely cover the chicken. Cover the Ninja Foodi PossibleCooker and cook on high for about 3 hours, or on low for 6 hours, until the chicken is thoroughly cooked and an instant-read thermometer reads 165ºF (74ºC) when inserted into the thickest part of a thigh. Once done, transfer the chicken to a cutting board and cover it loosely with foil. 3. To prepare the rice, strain the broth, ensuring you have about 8 cups; set aside 2½ cups for later and reserve the remainder for another use. Skim off any fat from the broth's surface and transfer about 2 tablespoons of fat to a saucepan. Over high heat, sauté the garlic and ginger until fragrant, about 1 minute. Add the rice to the pan and stir to coat it with the fat. Pour in the reserved 2½ cups of broth and bring to a boil. Once boiling, cover the pan and reduce the heat to low, simmering until the liquid is absorbed, approximately 17 minutes. After cooking, let the rice stand for 5 minutes before fluffing it with a fork. 4. Carve the chicken into portions and slice it as desired. Thinly slice the reserved scallions and chop the remaining cilantro. Serve the chicken and rice on plates, garnishing with the chopped cilantro and scallions. Provide the broth on the side, and drizzle with chili oil for added flavor. Enjoy!

Creamy Turkey Tetrazzini Bake

Prep time: 20 minutes | Cook time: 6 hours | Serves 4

- Cooking spray or 1 tablespoon extra-virgin olive oil
- 3 cups diced cooked turkey
- 1 small onion, finely chopped
- 2 cups low-sodium chicken stock
- 1 cup heavy (whipping) cream
- 2 tablespoons dry sherry
- 1½ cups grated Parmesan cheese, plus more for garnish
- 4 ounces (113 g) cream cheese
- 1 teaspoon kosher salt, plus more for seasoning
- ½ teaspoon freshly ground black pepper, plus more for seasoning
- ⅛ teaspoon ground nutmeg
- 1 cup frozen peas

1. Use the cooking spray or olive oil to coat the inside (bottom and sides) of the Ninja Foodi PossibleCooker. Add the turkey, onion, chicken stock, heavy cream, sherry, Parmesan, cream cheese, salt, pepper, and nutmeg. Stir to combine. Cover and cook on low for 6 hours. 2. About 25 minutes before serving, add the peas. Season with additional salt and pepper, as needed. When the peas have finished cooking, serve and garnish with extra grated Parmesan.

Creamy Scalloped Chicken and Potato Medley

Prep time: 5 minutes | Cook time: 4 to 10 hours | Serves 4

- 1 (5-ounce / 142-g) package scalloped potatoes
- Scalloped potatoes dry seasoning pack
- 4 chicken breast halves or 8 legs
- 1 (10-ounce / 283-g) package frozen peas
- 2 cups water

1. Put potatoes, seasoning pack, chicken, and peas in Ninja Foodi PossibleCooker. Pour water over all. 2. Cover. Cook on low 8 to 10 hours, or on high 4 hours.

Chicken Balsamico with Yukon Gold Potatoes

Prep time: 15 minutes | Cook time: 3 to 6 hours | Serves 6 to 8

- 6 medium Yukon gold potatoes, quartered
- 8 strips bacon, cut into ½-inch pieces
- 8 chicken thighs, skin removed
- Salt and freshly ground black pepper
- 2 tablespoons finely chopped fresh rosemary
- 8 cloves garlic, quartered
- 1 cup balsamic vinegar
- ½ cup chicken broth
- Salt and freshly ground black pepper

1. Begin by placing the potatoes into the insert of a 5- to 7-quart Ninja Foodi PossibleCooker. In a large skillet, cook the bacon over medium heat until it becomes crispy. Once done, remove the bacon and place it on paper towels to drain, leaving the drippings in the skillet. 2. Season the chicken evenly with 1½ teaspoons of salt and ½ teaspoon of pepper, then add it to the skillet with the bacon drippings. 3. Brown the chicken on all sides for about 12 to 15 minutes. After browning, add the rosemary and garlic, sautéing for an additional 1 to 2 minutes. Deglaze the skillet with vinegar, scraping up any browned bits from the bottom, and transfer everything to the Ninja Foodi PossibleCooker. 4. Pour the broth over the chicken and potatoes in the Ninja Foodi PossibleCooker. Cover and cook on high for 3 hours or on low for 5 to 6 hours, until both the chicken and potatoes are tender. Taste and adjust seasoning with salt and pepper as needed. 5. Before serving, sprinkle the reserved crispy bacon over the chicken and potatoes for added flavor and crunch. Enjoy!

Teriyaki-Style Pacific Chicken Thighs

Prep time: 10 minutes | Cook time: 7 to 8 hours | Serves 6

- 6 to 8 skinless chicken thighs
- ½ cup soy sauce
- 2 tablespoons brown sugar
- 2 tablespoons grated fresh ginger
- 2 garlic cloves, minced

1. Wash and dry chicken. Place in Ninja Foodi PossibleCooker. 2. Combine remaining ingredients. Pour over chicken. 3. Cover. Cook on high 1 hour. Reduce heat to low and cook 6 to 7 hours. 4. Serve.

Chicken Breasts in Port Wine Smothered with Leeks

Prep time: 15 minutes | Cook time: 3 hours | Serves 6

- 4 tablespoons (½ stick) unsalted butter
- 4 large leeks, finely chopped, using the white and tender green parts
- Salt and freshly ground black pepper
- 6 chicken breast halves, boned and skinned
- 1 cup Ruby Port
- ½ cup double-strength chicken broth
- ½ cup heavy cream

1. In a large skillet, melt the butter over medium-high heat. Add the leeks, seasoning them with ½ teaspoon of salt and ¼ teaspoon of pepper. Sauté for 2 to 3 minutes until the leeks become fragrant. Transfer the sautéed leeks to the insert of a 5- to 7-quart Ninja Foodi PossibleCooker. 2. Season the chicken breasts with 1 teaspoon of salt and ¼ teaspoon of pepper, then place them on top of the leeks in the Ninja Foodi PossibleCooker. Pour in the port and broth, ensuring everything is well combined. Cover the Ninja Foodi PossibleCooker and cook on low for 3 hours, or until the chicken is cooked through and tender. 3. Once cooked, transfer the chicken to a serving platter and cover it with aluminum foil to keep warm. Pour the leeks and cooking liquid into a saucepan and bring it to a boil over medium heat. Let it boil for 5 minutes, then stir in the cream and adjust seasoning with additional salt and pepper, if desired. 4. Slice each chicken breast diagonally into four pieces. On each plate, ladle some of the leek sauce, place the chicken on top, and drizzle with the remaining sauce. Enjoy your flavorful dish!

Turkey Meat Loaf

Prep time: 15 minutes | Cook time: 6 to 8 hours | Serves 8

- 1½ pounds (680 g) lean ground turkey
- 2 egg whites
- ⅓ cup ketchup
- 1 tablespoon Worcestershire sauce
- 1 teaspoon dried basil
- ½ teaspoon salt
- ½ teaspoon black pepper
- 2 small onions, chopped
- 2 potatoes, finely shredded
- 2 small red bell peppers, finely chopped

1. In a large mixing bowl, combine all the ingredients thoroughly, ensuring everything is evenly mixed. 2. Form the mixture into a loaf shape that fits comfortably in your Ninja Foodi PossibleCooker. Carefully place the shaped loaf into the Ninja Foodi PossibleCooker. 3. Cover the Ninja Foodi PossibleCooker with the lid and cook on low for 6 to 8 hours, allowing the flavors to meld and the meatloaf to cook through. Serve warm.

Lemon-Dill Spinach Feta Stuffed Chicken Breasts

Prep time: 20 minutes | Cook time: 5 hours | Serves 6

Stuffed Chicken:

- 4 tablespoons olive oil
- 2 tablespoons finely chopped shallot
- 1 garlic clove, minced
- 3½ pounds (1.6 kg) fresh spinach (or 1 pound / 454 g frozen, thawed)
- 1 teaspoon sea salt

Lemon-Dill Sauce:

- 2 tablespoons unsalted butter
- 2 tablespoons all-purpose flour
- 1½ cups chicken stock
- 1 cup heavy cream
- ½ teaspoon black pepper
- ¼ teaspoon ground nutmeg
- 1 cup crumbled feta cheese
- 6 boneless, skinless chicken breast halves
- ½ cup dry white wine
- 2 cups chicken stock

- Zest of 1 lemon
- 2 tablespoons fresh lemon juice
- ¼ cup chopped fresh dill
- Sea salt
- Black pepper

Make the Stuffed Chicken: 1. In a large skillet, heat the olive oil over medium-high heat. Add the shallot and garlic and sauté for 2 minutes, or until the shallot is slightly softened. 2. Add the spinach, 1 teaspoon salt, ½ teaspoon black pepper, and the nutmeg to the skillet. Sauté the spinach until the liquid in the pan has evaporated and the spinach is dry. Remove to a medium bowl, cool the mixture slightly, and stir in the feta cheese. Set aside. 3. On a cutting board, spread out a piece of parchment paper as large as the board. Trim the chicken breasts of any excess fat, and lay one breast shiny-side (skin-side) down on the parchment paper. Place another piece of parchment paper over the chicken, and pound with a meat pounder, flat-bottom bottle, or rolling pin to an even thickness, about ½ inch. Repeat with the 5 remaining chicken breast halves. 4. Lay a chicken breast half on the work surface and season with salt and pepper. Place about 2 tablespoons of the spinach-feta filling in the center of the breast. Roll up the breast, beginning at the widest end and tucking in the sides, and secure with a toothpick. Repeat with the remaining chicken breasts and filling. 5. In the skillet over medium-high heat, brown the stuffed chicken breasts in the remaining olive oil in batches, transferring them to the Ninja Foodi PossibleCooker when they are browned around all sides. 6. Add the wine to the skillet, scraping up the flavorful browned bits from the bottom of the pan. Pour the wine and the chicken stock into the Ninja Foodi PossibleCooker. 7. Cover and cook on high for 2½ hours or on low for 4 to 5 hours, until the chicken is cooked through and registers 160°F (71°C) on a meat thermometer. 8. Using tongs, remove the chicken from the Ninja Foodi PossibleCooker, arrange on a cutting board, and cover with parchment paper. Allow the chicken to rest for 5 minutes. Cut each chicken breast half on the bias into three pieces, and serve in a pool of the lemon-dill sauce. Make the Lemon-Dill Sauce: 1. In a medium skillet, melt the butter over medium heat. Whisk in the flour. Cook, whisking constantly. When white bubbles form, cook for another 2 to 3 minutes, still whisking. 2. Gradually add the broth, whisking until it comes to a boil and the mixture is smooth and thickened. 3. Stir in the cream, lemon zest, lemon juice, and dill. Season with salt and pepper. 4. Serve hot, or cool to room temperature and refrigerate for up to 4 days. Gently reheat over low heat before serving.

Creamy Paprika Hungarian Chicken Thighs

Prep time: 10 minutes | Cook time: 7 to 8 hours | Serves 4

- 1 tablespoon extra-virgin olive oil
- 2 pounds (907 g) boneless chicken thighs
- ½ cup chicken broth
- Juice and zest of 1 lemon
- 2 teaspoons minced garlic
- 2 teaspoons paprika
- ¼ teaspoon salt
- 1 cup sour cream
- 1 tablespoon chopped parsley, for garnish

1. Lightly grease the insert of the Ninja Foodi PossibleCooker with the olive oil. 2. Place the chicken thighs in the insert. 3. In a small bowl, stir together the broth, lemon juice and zest, garlic, paprika, and salt. Pour the broth mixture over the chicken. 4. Cover and cook on low for 7 to 8 hours. 5. Turn off the heat and stir in the sour cream. 6. Serve topped with the parsley.

Chicken Korma

Marinade:

- 1 tablespoon coriander seeds, ground
- 1 teaspoon salt
- 6 whole black peppercorns
- 1-inch piece fresh ginger, roughly chopped
- 3 garlic cloves, roughly chopped

Korma:

- 1 tablespoon ghee or vegetable oil
- 3 cloves
- 3 green cardamom pods
- 1-inch piece cassia bark
- 1 to 3 dried red chiles
- 2 onions, minced
- ⅓ cup creamed coconut
- 2 heaped tablespoons ground almonds

- 12 boneless chicken thighs, skinned and chopped into chunks
- 1 cup Greek yogurt
- 1 heaped teaspoon gram flour
- 1 teaspoon turmeric

- 1 teaspoon ground white poppy seeds
- Pinch of saffron
- 2 tablespoons milk
- 1 teaspoon garam masala
- Handful fresh coriander leaves, finely chopped
- 1 tablespoon chopped toasted almonds
- Squeeze of lemon juice

1. Begin by preparing the marinade: in a mortar and pestle, combine coriander seeds, salt, and peppercorns, crushing them finely. Alternatively, use a spice grinder for this step. Next, incorporate the chopped ginger and garlic, pounding them together until a fragrant paste forms. 2. In a spacious mixing bowl, add the chicken along with yogurt, gram flour, turmeric, and the spice paste. Mix well to ensure the chicken is evenly coated. Cover the bowl and let it marinate in the refrigerator for at least an hour, preferably longer for enhanced flavor. 3. Now, let's move on to making the Korma: set your Ninja Foodi PossibleCooker to the high setting and pour in the oil. Introduce the cloves, cardamom pods, cassia bark, and dried red chiles, toasting them for about a minute until they release their aroma. 4. Add the minced onions and stir them in before adding the marinated chicken. Secure the lid and let it cook on low for two hours or on high for one hour. 5. After this initial cooking time, mix in the creamed coconut, ground almonds, and poppy seeds, stirring well to combine. Cover the cooker again and let it cook on low for another two hours. 6. For an added touch of luxury, crumble saffron into a small bowl, pour in some milk, and allow it to steep for 20 minutes. 7. Once the Korma is thoroughly cooked and the sauce has thickened, incorporate the saffron milk if desired, followed by the garam masala. Finish by garnishing with fresh coriander leaves and chopped almonds. A squeeze of lemon juice can be added for a refreshing twist. Serve the Korma warm and enjoy!

Classic Chicken Pot Pie with Hearty Vegetables

- 3 cups chicken broth
- 1 teaspoon dried thyme
- 4 medium Yukon gold potatoes, cut into ½-inch cubes
- 2 cups baby carrots
- 4 cups cooked chicken, cut into bite-size pieces or shredded

- 1½ cups frozen petite peas, defrosted
- 1 cup frozen white corn, defrosted
- 2 tablespoons unsalted butter, at room temperature
- 2 tablespoons all-purpose flour

1. Pour the broth in the insert of a 5- to 7-quart Ninja Foodi PossibleCooker. Add the thyme, potatoes, and carrots, and stir to combine. Cover and cook on high for 3 to 4 hours, until the potatoes are tender. 2. Add the chicken, peas and corn and stir to combine. In a small bowl, stir the butter and flour and make a paste. Add the paste to the Ninja Foodi PossibleCooker and stir to combine. Cover and cook for an additional 45 minutes to 1 hour, until the sauce is thickened. 3. Serve from the cooker set on warm.

Tea "Smoked" Turkey Legs

- 2 cups chicken broth
- 8 bags Lapsang Souchong or black tea
- 4 slices fresh ginger

- 1 cinnamon stick
- ½ cup soy sauce
- ¼ cup hoisin sauce
- 6 turkey legs, skin removed

1. Start by boiling the broth in a saucepan, then introduce the tea bags, ginger, and cinnamon. Allow the mixture to cool for about 45 minutes. Once cooled, strain the broth using a fine-mesh sieve into a bowl, and whisk in the soy sauce and hoisin sauce until well combined. 2. Using a silicone pastry brush, apply some of the sauce onto the turkey legs. Pour the remaining sauce into the insert of a 5- to 7-quart Ninja Foodi PossibleCooker. Place the rack inside the Ninja Foodi PossibleCooker and arrange the turkey legs on top of it. 3. Cover the Ninja Foodi PossibleCooker and set it to high, cooking for 5 hours while basting the turkey legs a few times throughout the cooking process. 4. Once the cooking time is complete, slice the turkey legs into individual serving pieces and serve them warm. Enjoy your flavorful turkey dish!

Spicy Tomato-Peanut Chicken Breasts

Prep time: 15 minutes | Cook time: 3 to 8 hours | Serves 6

- 6 bone-in chicken breast halves
- 2 (14½-ounce / 411-g) cans diced tomatoes, undrained
- 1 small can jalapeños, sliced and drained (optional)
- ¼ cup reduced-fat, creamy peanut butter
- 2 tablespoons fresh cilantro, chopped (optional)
- Nonfat cooking spray

1. Remove skin from chicken, but leave bone in. 2. Mix all ingredients, except chicken, in medium-sized bowl. 3. Pour one-third of sauce in bottom of Ninja Foodi PossibleCooker sprayed with nonfat cooking spray. Place chicken on top. 4. Pour remaining sauce over chicken. 5. Cover. Cook on high 3 to 4 hours, or on low 6 to 8 hours. 6. Remove from Ninja Foodi PossibleCooker gently. Chicken will be very tender and will fall off the bones.

Catalan Chicken with Spiced Lemon Rice

Prep time: 30 minutes | Cook time: 5 hours | Serves 4

- 3 tablespoons all-purpose flour
- 2 tablespoons paprika
- 1 tablespoon garlic powder
- Sea salt
- Black pepper
- 6 chicken thighs
- ¼ cup olive oil
- 1 (15-ounce / 425-g) can diced tomatoes, with the juice
- 2 green bell peppers, diced into 2-inch pieces
- 1 large yellow onion, sliced into thick pieces
- 2 tablespoons tomato paste
- 4 cups chicken stock
- 1 cup uncooked brown rice
- ½ teaspoon red pepper flakes
- Zest and juice from 1 lemon
- ½ cup pitted green olives

1. In a large resealable bag, mix together the flour, paprika, and garlic powder and season with salt and pepper. Add the chicken, reseal the bag, and toss to coat. 2. In a large skillet over medium heat, heat the olive oil. Add the chicken and brown on both sides, 3 to 4 minutes per side. 3. While the chicken is cooking, add the tomatoes, bell peppers, and onion to the Ninja Foodi PossibleCooker. 4. Place the browned chicken thighs in the Ninja Foodi PossibleCooker. 5. In same skillet used to brown the chicken, add the tomato paste and cook for 1 minute, stirring constantly.

6. Add 2 cups of the chicken stock to the skillet and bring to a simmer, stirring with a wooden spoon to scrape up the flavorful browned bits off the bottom of the pan. Pour over the top of the chicken in the Ninja Foodi PossibleCooker. 7. Cook on low for 4 hours, or until the chicken is extremely tender. 8. In a heavy medium saucepan over medium-high heat, combine the remaining 2 cups stock, the rice, red pepper flakes, lemon zest, and juice of one-half of the lemon, and season with salt. Bring to a boil, reduce the heat to low, and simmer, covered, until the rice is tender and has absorbed all the liquid, about 25 minutes. 9. To serve, spoon the rice onto plates and ladle the Catalonian chicken and vegetables over the top. Garnish with the olives and squeeze the juice from the remaining one-half lemon over the dish.

Crispy Vietnamese-Style Chicken Wings with Sweet Sauce

Prep time: 25 minutes | Cook time: 3 hours | Serves 8

- 3 pounds (1.4 kg) chicken wing drumettes
- ¼ cup olive oil

Sauce:

- 2 tablespoons vegetable oil
- 1 medium onion, cut into half rounds
- ½ cup ketchup
- ¼ cup soy sauce
- ½ cup firmly packed light brown sugar
- 2 cloves garlic, minced
- 1½ teaspoons salt
- 1 teaspoon sweet paprika
- Freshly ground black pepper
- 1 teaspoon freshly grated ginger
- 1 teaspoon ground coriander
- 2 tablespoons Asian fish sauce (Nuoc Nam)
- ½ cup chicken broth
- ½ cup finely chopped fresh cilantro, for garnish

1. Coat the insert of of a 5- to 7-quart Ninja Foodi PossibleCooker with nonstick cooking spray. Preheat the broiler for 10 minutes. 2. Put the wings, olive oil, salt, paprika, and a generous grinding of pepper in a large mixing bowl and toss until the wings are evenly coated. Arrange the wings on a wire rack in a baking sheet and broil until the wings are crispy on one side, about 5 minutes. 3. Turn the wings and broil until crispy and browned, an additional 5 minutes. 4. Remove the wings from the oven. If you would like to do this step ahead of time, cool the wings and refrigerate for up to 2 days. Otherwise, put the wings in the prepared cooker insert. 5. Combine all the sauce ingredients in a mixing bowl and stir. Pour the sauce over the wings and turn to coat. 6. Cover and cook for on high for 3 hours, turning the wings several times to coat in the sauce. 7. Garnish the wings with the cilantro and serve from the cooker set on warm.

Cashew Chicken and Snap Peas

Prep time: 15 minutes | Cook time: 6 hours | Serves 2

- 16 ounces (454 g) boneless, skinless chicken breasts, cut into 2-inch pieces
- 2 cups sugar snap peas, strings removed
- 1 teaspoon grated fresh ginger
- 1 teaspoon minced garlic
- 2 tablespoons low-sodium soy sauce
- 1 tablespoon ketchup
- 1 tablespoon rice vinegar
- 1 teaspoon honey
- Pinch red pepper flakes
- ¼ cup toasted cashews
- 1 scallion, white and green parts, sliced thin

1. Place the chicken and sugar snap peas in the Ninja Foodi PossibleCooker, ensuring they are evenly distributed. 2. In a measuring cup or small bowl, whisk together the ginger, garlic, soy sauce, ketchup, vinegar, honey, and red pepper flakes until well combined. Pour this flavorful mixture over the chicken and snap peas, coating them thoroughly. 3. Cover the Ninja Foodi PossibleCooker and cook on low for 6 hours, until the chicken is fully cooked and the snap peas are tender but still crisp. 4. Just before serving, gently stir in the cashews and sliced scallions for added crunch and freshness. Enjoy your delicious meal!

Tex-Mex Chicken and Beans

Prep time: 20 minutes | Cook time: 8 hours | Serves 4

- 1 cup dried pinto beans, rinsed
- 1 (11-ounce / 312-g) jar mild or medium salsa (1½ cups)
- 2 tablespoons chopped chipotle chile in adobo sauce
- 2 tablespoons all-purpose flour
- 1 cup water
- 1½ pounds (680 g) boneless, skinless chicken thighs (about 8)
- Coarse salt and freshly ground pepper
- 1 red onion, chopped
- 1 red bell pepper, chopped
- Sour cream, finely chopped jalapeño, hot sauce, and tortilla strips or chips, for serving

1. In a large bowl, place the beans and cover them with several inches of water. Refrigerate overnight, ensuring the bowl is covered, then drain the beans. 2. Preheat your 5- to 6-quart Ninja Foodi PossibleCooker. 3. Add the drained beans, salsa, chiles, flour, and water to the Ninja Foodi PossibleCooker, stirring to combine everything well. Season the chicken with salt and pepper, then place it on top of the bean mixture. Scatter the chopped onion and bell pepper over the chicken. 4. Cover the Ninja Foodi PossibleCooker and cook on low for 8 hours, or on high for 4 hours, until the chicken is fully cooked. 5. Once cooked, transfer the chicken to a large plate and use two forks to shred it into large pieces. Return the shredded chicken to the stew and mix it in. Serve the stew with optional toppings such as sour cream, jalapeños, hot sauce, and tortilla strips. Enjoy!

Chettinad Chicken

Prep time: 15 minutes | Cook time: 4 to 6 hours | Serves 6

- 1 tablespoon white poppy seeds
- 1 teaspoon coriander seeds
- 2 teaspoons cumin seeds
- 1 teaspoon fennel seeds
- 4 to 5 dried red chiles
- 2-inch piece cinnamon stick
- 6 green cardamom pods
- 4 cloves
- 1½ cups grated coconut
- 4 garlic cloves
- 1 tablespoon freshly grated ginger
- 2 tablespoons coconut oil
- 20 curry leaves
- 3 onions, finely sliced
- 2 star anise
- 4 tomatoes
- 1 teaspoon turmeric
- Sea salt
- 1 teaspoon chili powder
- 12 chicken thighs on the bone, skinned and trimmed
- Juice of 2 or 3 limes
- Handful fresh coriander leaves, chopped

1. In a frying pan over medium heat, toast the poppy seeds, coriander seeds, cumin seeds, fennel seeds, dried red chiles, cinnamon stick, green cardamom pods, and cloves for about 1 minute or until they become fragrant. Remove from heat and let them cool. Once cooled, grind the mixture into a fine powder using a spice grinder. 2. In the same frying pan, add the grated coconut and toast it for 3 to 4 minutes, stirring frequently until it just begins to turn golden brown. Remove it from the pan and spread it on a plate to cool. After it cools, grind the toasted coconut and mix it with the ground spice blend. 3. Using a mortar and pestle, crush the garlic and ginger together and set aside. 4. Either set the Ninja Foodi PossibleCooker to the sauté function or heat a pan on the stove. Add the coconut oil and heat it. Once hot, toss in the curry leaves. When the leaves stop spluttering, add the sliced onions and sauté until they turn light brown. Stir in the crushed garlic and ginger, cooking for another minute or two until fragrant. 5. Transfer the onion mixture to the Ninja Foodi PossibleCooker, then add the ground spices and star anise. Chop the tomatoes and add them along with the turmeric and salt, then stir in the chili powder. 6. Place the chicken pieces into the Ninja Foodi PossibleCooker, cover, and cook on low for 6 hours or on high for 4 hours, until the chicken is tender and thoroughly cooked. 7. Before serving, check the seasoning and adjust as necessary. Squeeze in some lime juice and garnish with fresh coriander leaves for added flavor. Enjoy your dish!

Lemon Herb Chicken One-Pot

- 6 to 8 potatoes, quartered
- 1 to 2 large onions, sliced
- 3 to 5 carrots, cubed
- 1 (5-pound / 2.3-kg) chicken, skin removed
- 1 small onion, chopped
- 1 teaspoon black pepper
- 1 tablespoon whole cloves
- 1 tablespoon garlic salt
- 1 tablespoon chopped fresh oregano
- 1 teaspoon dried rosemary
- ½ cup lemon juice or chicken broth

1. Layer potatoes, sliced onions, and carrots in bottom of Ninja Foodi PossibleCooker. 2. Rinse and pat chicken dry. In bowl mix together chopped onions, pepper, cloves, and garlic salt. Dredge chicken in seasonings. Place in cooker over vegetables. Spoon any remaining seasonings over chicken. 3. Sprinkle with oregano and rosemary. Pour lemon juice over chicken. 4. Cover. Cook on low 6 hours.

Savory Asian Chicken and Napa Cabbage Rolls

- 1 head Napa cabbage
- 2 cups chicken broth
- ½ cup soy sauce
- 4 slices fresh ginger
- 2 tablespoons vegetable oil
- 2 cloves garlic, minced
- 1 teaspoon freshly grated ginger
- 6 canned water chestnuts, finely chopped
- 2 chicken breast halves, skin and bones removed, finely chopped
- 4 green onions, finely chopped, using the white and tender green parts
- 2 tablespoons hoisin sauce
- 1 tablespoon cornstarch mixed with 2 tablespoons water

1. Core the cabbage and separate the leaves, being careful not to tear them. Put the broth, soy sauce, and ginger in a large stockpot and bring to a boil. 2. Blanch the cabbage leaves, one at a time, for 30 seconds until limp. Drain the leaves and set aside. Add the broth mixture to the insert of a 5- to 7-quart Ninja Foodi PossibleCooker. Cover and set on warm while preparing the filling. 3. Heat the oil in a sauté pan over high heat. Add the garlic, ginger, and water chestnuts and sauté for 30 seconds. Add the chicken and cook until the chicken turns white, 3 to 5 minutes. 4. Transfer the contents of the pan to a bowl and stir in the green onions and hoisin sauce. Place 2 to 3 tablespoons of filling at the stem end of a cabbage leaf and roll up, tucking in the sides of the leaf as you go. Place the cabbage wraps on a rack in the Ninja Foodi PossibleCooker. 5. Cover and cook on high for 1½ to 2 hours, until the chicken is cooked through. Remove the wraps and set aside. Strain the broth through a fine-mesh sieve into a saucepan and bring to a boil. Add the cornstarch mixture and bring back to a boil. 6. Serve the wraps with the sauce on the side.

Herb-Seasoned Turkey Breast with Avocado Salsa

- 3 tablespoons extra-virgin olive oil, divided
- 1½ pounds (680 g) boneless turkey breasts
- Salt, for seasoning
- Freshly ground black pepper, for seasoning
- 1 cup coconut milk
- 2 teaspoons minced garlic
- 2 teaspoons dried thyme
- 1 teaspoon dried oregano
- 1 avocado, peeled, pitted, and chopped
- 1 tomato, diced
- ½ jalapeño pepper, diced
- 1 tablespoon chopped cilantro

1. Lightly grease the insert of the Ninja Foodi PossibleCooker with 1 tablespoon of the olive oil. 2. In a large skillet over medium-high heat, heat the remaining 2 tablespoons of the olive oil. 3. Lightly season the turkey with salt and pepper. Add the turkey to the skillet and brown for about 7 minutes, turning once. 4. Transfer the turkey to the insert and add the coconut milk, garlic, thyme, and oregano. 5. Cover and cook on low for 7 to 8 hours. 6. In a small bowl, stir together the avocado, tomato, jalapeño pepper, and cilantro. 7. Serve the turkey topped with the avocado salsa.

Mulligan Stew

Prep time: 15 minutes | Cook time: 7 hours | Serves 8 to 10

- 1 (3-pound / 1.4-kg) stewing hen, cut up, or 4 pounds (1.8 kg) chicken legs and thighs
- 1½ teaspoons salt
- 1 (¼-pound / 113-g) salt pork or bacon, cut in 1-inch squares
- 4 cups tomatoes, peeled and sliced
- 2 cups fresh corn, or 1
- (1-pound / 454-g) package frozen corn
- 1 cup coarsely chopped potatoes
- 1 (10-ounce / 283-g) package lima beans, frozen
- ½ cup chopped onions
- 1 teaspoon salt
- ¼ teaspoon pepper
- Dash of cayenne pepper

1. Place the chicken in a very large Ninja Foodi PossibleCooker and add enough water to cover it completely. Sprinkle in 1½ teaspoons of salt to season. 2. Cover the Ninja Foodi PossibleCooker and cook on low for 2 hours, checking occasionally to add more water if necessary to keep the chicken submerged. 3. After 2 hours, add the remaining ingredients to the Ninja Foodi PossibleCooker. If your Ninja Foodi PossibleCooker isn't large enough, divide the stew between two average-sized Ninja Foodi PossibleCookers. Cover and simmer on low for an additional 5 hours, allowing the flavors to meld and the chicken to become tender. Enjoy your hearty stew!

Pesto Chicken with Stewed Vegetables

Prep time: 15 minutes | Cook time: 6 to 8 hours | Serves 2

- 1 zucchini, cut into 1-inch pieces
- 1 cup grape tomatoes
- 1 red bell pepper, cored and sliced thin
- ½ red onion, halved and sliced thin
- 1 tablespoon assorted fresh herbs
- 1 teaspoon extra-virgin olive oil
- ⅛ teaspoon sea salt
- Freshly ground black pepper
- 2 bone-in, skinless chicken thighs, about 8 ounces (227 g) each
- ¼ cup pesto

1. In the Ninja Foodi PossibleCooker, combine the zucchini, grape tomatoes, red bell pepper, onion, and herbs, stirring gently to mix everything together. Drizzle the vegetables with olive oil and season with salt and a few grinds of black pepper. 2. In a separate medium bowl, coat the chicken thoroughly with pesto on all sides. Once coated, place the chicken on top of the vegetable mixture in the Ninja Foodi PossibleCooker. 3. Cover the Ninja Foodi PossibleCooker and cook on low for 6 to 8 hours, or until the vegetables are very tender and the chicken is fully cooked. Enjoy your delicious, healthy meal!

Thai Peanut Wings

Prep time: 20 minutes | Cook time: 3 hours | Serves 8

- 3 pounds (1.4 kg) chicken wing drumettes
- ¼ cup olive oil

Sauce:

- 1 (14-ounce / 397-g) can coconut milk
- ½ cup chicken broth
- 1 cup smooth peanut butter
- ¼ cup firmly packed brown sugar
- 2 tablespoons soy sauce
- 1½ teaspoons salt
- 1 teaspoon sweet paprika
- Freshly ground black pepper
- 2 teaspoons freshly grated ginger
- ¼ teaspoon hot sauce
- ½ cup finely chopped fresh cilantro, for garnish
- ½ cup finely chopped roasted peanuts, for garnish

1. Begin by spraying the insert of a 5- to 7-quart Ninja Foodi PossibleCooker with nonstick cooking spray. Preheat your broiler for 10 minutes to ensure it's hot. 2. In a large mixing bowl, combine the wings, olive oil, salt, paprika, and a generous amount of freshly ground pepper. Toss everything together until the wings are well coated. Place the wings on a wire rack set over a baking sheet and broil for approximately 5 minutes until crispy on one side. 3. Flip the wings over and continue broiling for an additional 5 minutes until they are crispy and browned all over. 4. Once done, remove the wings from the oven. If you prefer to prepare this step in advance, allow the wings to cool, then refrigerate them for up to 2 days. Otherwise, transfer the wings to the prepared Ninja Foodi PossibleCooker insert. 5. In a small saucepan, combine all the ingredients for the sauce and place it over medium heat, stirring to mix. 6. Bring the sauce to a boil, then pour it over the wings, making sure to turn them to coat evenly. 7. Cover the Ninja Foodi PossibleCooker and set it to high, cooking for 3 hours while turning the wings occasionally to ensure they are well coated in the sauce. 8. When ready to serve, garnish the wings with fresh cilantro and peanuts, then serve them warm directly from the cooker. Enjoy your delicious wings!

Chapter 6

Fish and Seafood

Chapter 6 Fish and Seafood

Simple Poached Turbot

Prep time: 10 minutes | Cook time: 40 to 50 minutes | Serves 4

- 1 cup vegetable or chicken stock
- ½ cup dry white wine
- 1 yellow onion, sliced
- 1 lemon, sliced
- 4 sprigs fresh dill
- ½ teaspoon sea salt
- 4 (6-ounce / 170-g) turbot fillets

1. Pour the stock and wine into the Ninja Foodi PossibleCooker. Cover and heat on high for 20 to 30 minutes, allowing the liquid to warm up thoroughly. 2. Add the sliced onion, lemon slices, chopped dill, a pinch of salt, and the turbot fillets into the Ninja Foodi PossibleCooker. Cover again and cook on high for about 20 minutes, or until the turbot turns opaque and is cooked to your preferred doneness. Serve immediately while hot.

Spicy Creole Crayfish Stew

Prep time: 15 minutes | Cook time: 3 to 8 hours | Serves 2

- 1½ cups diced celery
- 1 large yellow onion, chopped
- 2 small bell peppers, any colors, chopped
- 1 (8-ounce / 227-g) can tomato sauce
- 1 (28-ounce / 794-g) can whole tomatoes, broken up,
- with the juice
- 1 clove garlic, minced
- 1 teaspoon sea salt
- ¼ teaspoon black pepper
- 6 drops hot pepper sauce (like Tabasco)
- 1 pound (454 g) precooked crayfish meat

1. Place the celery, onion, and bell peppers in the Ninja Foodi PossibleCooker. Add the tomato sauce, tomatoes, and garlic. Sprinkle with the salt and pepper and add the hot sauce. 2. Cover and cook on high for 3 to 4 hours or on low for 6 to 8 hours. 3. About 30 minutes before the cooking time is completed, add the crayfish. 4. Serve hot.

Seafood Stew

Prep time: 15 minutes | Cook time: 6 hours | Serves 8

- 1 pound (454 g) waxy baby potatoes, such as Yukon Gold
- 2 medium onions, finely chopped
- 2 celery stalks, finely chopped
- 5 garlic cloves, minced
- 1 (28-ounce / 794-g) can crushed tomatoes
- 1 (8-ounce / 227-g) bottle clam juice
- 8 ounces (227 g) low-sodium fish stock
- 1 (6-ounce / 170-g) can tomato paste
- 1 tablespoon balsamic vinegar
- 1 teaspoon sugar
- ½ teaspoon celery salt
- ½ teaspoon kosher salt, plus more for seasoning
- ½ teaspoon freshly ground black pepper, plus more for seasoning
- 2 bay leaves
- 1 pound (454 g) firm-fleshed white fish, such as cod, cut into 1-inch pieces
- ½ pound (227 g) medium uncooked shrimp, shelled and deveined
- ½ pound (227 g) scallops, small side muscle removed, halved
- ¼ cup finely chopped flat-leaf parsley, for garnish

1. Place the potatoes, onions, celery, minced garlic, diced tomatoes, clam juice, fish stock, tomato paste, vinegar, sugar, celery salt, kosher salt, black pepper, and bay leaves into the Ninja Foodi PossibleCooker. Mix well to combine all the ingredients. Cover the Ninja Foodi PossibleCooker and set it to low, letting it cook for 6 hours, or until the potatoes are soft and easily pierced with a fork. 2. Roughly 30 minutes before the stew is ready to serve, add the white fish fillets, shrimp, and scallops to the Ninja Foodi PossibleCooker. Cover again and continue cooking on low until the seafood is fully cooked and tender. 3. Remove and discard the bay leaves from the stew. Taste and adjust seasoning with additional salt and pepper if necessary. Ladle the hot stew into bowls, sprinkle freshly chopped parsley over the top, and serve immediately.

Creamy Smoked Salmon and Potato Bake

Prep time: 10 minutes | Cook time: 8 hours | Serves 2

- 1 teaspoon butter, at room temperature, or extra-virgin olive oil
- 2 eggs
- 1 cup 2% milk
- 1 teaspoon dried dill
- ⅛ teaspoon sea salt
- Freshly ground black pepper
- 2 medium russet potatoes, peeled and sliced thin
- 4 ounces (113 g) smoked salmon

1. Grease the inside of the Ninja Foodi PossibleCooker with the butter. 2. In a small bowl, whisk together the eggs, milk, dill, salt, and a few grinds of the black pepper. 3. Spread one-third of the potatoes in a single layer on the bottom of the Ninja Foodi PossibleCooker and top them with one-third of the salmon. Pour one-third of the egg mixture over the salmon. Repeat this layering with the remaining potatoes, salmon, and egg mixture. 4. Cover and cook on low for 8 hours or overnight.

Poached Salmon Provenç

Prep time: 15 minutes | Cook time: 1½ to 2 hours | Serves 6

- 3 pounds (1.4 kg) salmon fillets
- ½ cup dry white wine or vermouth
- 4 cloves garlic, peeled
- 1½ teaspoons finely chopped fresh rosemary
- 2 teaspoons finely chopped fresh thyme leaves
- 2 teaspoons finely chopped fresh tarragon
- ½ cup olive oil
- 1 (28- to 32-ounce / 794- to 907-g) can plum tomatoes, drained
- ½ cup heavy cream
- Salt and freshly ground black pepper

1. Lay the salmon fillets in the insert of a 5- to 7-quart Ninja Foodi PossibleCooker and pour the white wine over them, ensuring the fish is partially submerged. 2. In a food processor, combine the garlic, rosemary, thyme, tarragon, olive oil, and tomatoes. Blend until the mixture becomes smooth, then spoon it generously over the salmon in the Ninja Foodi PossibleCooker. 3. Cover and cook on high for 1½ to 2 hours, or until the salmon is opaque and cooked through. 4. Carefully transfer the salmon from the Ninja Foodi PossibleCooker to a serving platter and remove the skin. Pour the sauce from the Ninja Foodi PossibleCooker into a saucepan and bring it to a boil, reducing it by about ¼ cup. Stir in the heavy cream, then season with salt and pepper to taste. 5. Serve the salmon hot, drizzling some of the creamy sauce over the top.

Tender Olive Oil-Poached Tuna Fillets

Prep time: 5 minutes | Cook time: 3 to 4 hours | Serves 6

- 3 pounds (1.4 kg) tuna fillets
- Olive oil to cover the fish
- 1 teaspoon coarse sea salt

1. Place the tuna in the insert of a 5- to 7-quart Ninja Foodi PossibleCooker and pour the oil over the tuna. The oil should cover the tuna, and depending on the shape of your Ninja Foodi PossibleCooker, you may need to add a bit more oil. Add the salt to the slow-cooker insert. 2. Cover and cook on low for 3 to 4 hours, until the tuna is cooked through and is white. Remove the tuna from the oil and cool completely before using.

Zesty Spicy Barbecued Scallops and Shrimp

Prep time: 20 minutes | Cook time: 1 hour | Serves 2

- ½ teaspoon paprika
- ½ teaspoon garlic powder
- ¼ teaspoon onion powder
- ¼ teaspoon cayenne pepper
- ¼ teaspoon dried oregano
- ¼ teaspoon dried thyme
- ½ teaspoon sea salt
- ½ teaspoon black pepper
- 2 cloves garlic, minced
- ½ cup olive oil
- ¼ cup Worcestershire sauce
- 1 tablespoon hot pepper sauce (like Tabasco)
- Juice of 1 lemon
- 1 pound (454 g) scallops
- 1 pound (454 g) large shrimp, unpeeled
- 1 green onion, finely chopped

1. Combine the paprika, garlic powder, onion powder, cayenne pepper, oregano, thyme, ½ teaspoon salt, and ¼ teaspoon black pepper. 2. Combine the paprika blend, garlic, olive oil, Worcestershire sauce, hot pepper sauce, and lemon juice in the Ninja Foodi PossibleCooker. Season with salt and pepper. 3. Cover and cook on high for 30 minutes or until hot. 4. Rinse the scallops and shrimp, and drain. 5. Spoon one-half of the sauce from the Ninja Foodi PossibleCooker into a glass measuring cup. 6. Place the scallops and shrimp in the Ninja Foodi PossibleCooker with the remaining sauce. Drizzle with the sauce in the measuring cup, and stir to coat. 7. Cover and cook on high for 30 minutes, until the scallops and shrimp are opaque. 8. Turn the heat to warm for serving. Sprinkle with the chopped green onion to serve.

Bayou Gulf Shrimp Gumbo

Prep time: 35 minutes | Cook time: 5 hours | Serves 6

- ½ pound (227 g) bacon strips, chopped
- 3 celery ribs, chopped
- 1 medium onion, chopped
- 1 medium green pepper, chopped
- 2 garlic cloves, minced
- 2 (8-ounce / 227-g) bottles clam juice
- 1 (14½-ounce / 411-g) can diced tomatoes, undrained
- 2 tablespoons Worcestershire sauce
- 1 teaspoon kosher salt
- 1 teaspoon dried marjoram
- 2 pounds (907 g) uncooked large shrimp, peeled and deveined
- 2½ cups frozen sliced okra, thawed
- Hot cooked rice

1. In a large skillet, cook the bacon over medium heat until it becomes crispy. Use a slotted spoon to transfer the bacon to paper towels to drain, reserving 2 tablespoons of the drippings in the skillet. Add the diced celery, chopped onion, green pepper, and minced garlic to the drippings, sautéing until the vegetables are tender. 2. Transfer the sautéed mixture into a 4-quart Ninja Foodi PossibleCooker. Add the cooked bacon, clam juice, diced tomatoes, Worcestershire sauce, salt, and marjoram, stirring to combine. Cover and cook on low for 4 hours to allow the flavors to develop. 3. Add the shrimp and sliced okra to the Ninja Foodi PossibleCooker, cover, and cook for an additional hour or until the shrimp turn pink and the okra is heated through. Serve hot with rice.

Zesty South-of-the-Border Halibut Bake

Prep time: 10 minutes | Cook time: 3½ hours | Serves 6

- 3 cups prepared medium-hot salsa
- 2 tablespoons fresh lime juice
- 1 teaspoon ground cumin
- 2 to 3 pounds (907 g to 1.4 kg) halibut fillets
- 1½ cup finely shredded Monterey Jack cheese (or Pepper Jack for a spicy topping)

1. Combine the salsa, lime juice, and cumin in the insert of a 5- to 7-quart Ninja Foodi PossibleCooker and stir. Cover the Ninja Foodi PossibleCooker and cook on low for 2 hours. 2. Put the halibut in the cooker and spoon some of the sauce over the top of the fish. Sprinkle the cheese evenly over the fish. Cover and cook for an additional 30 to 45 minutes. 3. Remove the halibut from the Ninja Foodi PossibleCooker and serve on a bed of the sauce.

Southern Low Country Seafood Feast

Prep time: 15 minutes | Cook time: 6 hours | Serves 8

- 8 medium red potatoes
- 2 large, sweet onions, such as Vidalia, quartered
- 2 pounds (907 g) smoked sausage, cut into 3-inch pieces
- 1 (3-ounce / 85-g) package seafood boil seasoning
- 1 (12-ounce / 340-g) bottle pale ale beer
- 10 cups water
- 4 ears of corn, halved
- 2 pounds (907 g) medium raw shrimp, shelled and deveined
- Cocktail sauce, for serving
- Hot sauce, for serving
- ½ cup melted butter, for serving
- 1 large lemon, cut into wedges, for garnish

1. In the Ninja Foodi PossibleCooker, put the potatoes, onions, smoked sausage, seafood boil seasoning, beer, and water. Stir to combine. Cover and cook for 6 hours, or until the potatoes are tender when pierced with a fork. 2. About 45 minutes before serving, add the corn. Cover and continue cooking for 25 minutes. Add the shrimp, cover, and continue cooking until the shrimp are pink and no longer translucent. 3. Drain the Ninja Foodi PossibleCooker, discard the cooking liquid, and serve the seafood with cocktail sauce, hot sauce, melted butter, and lemon wedges.

Zesty Citrus-Infused Swordfish Fillets

Prep time: 15 minutes | Cook time: 1½ hours | Serves 2

- Nonstick cooking oil spray
- 1½ pounds (680 g) swordfish fillets
- Sea salt
- Black pepper
- 1 yellow onion, chopped
- 5 tablespoons chopped fresh flat-leaf parsley
- 1 tablespoon olive oil
- 2 teaspoons lemon zest
- 2 teaspoons orange zest
- Orange and lemon slices, for garnish
- Fresh parsley sprigs, for garnish

1. Coat the interior of the Ninja Foodi PossibleCooker crock with nonstick cooking oil spray. 2. Season the fish fillets with salt and pepper. Place the fish in the Ninja Foodi PossibleCooker. 3. Distribute the onion, parsley, olive oil, lemon zest, and orange zest over fish. 4. Cover and cook on low for 1½ hours. 5. Serve hot, garnished with orange and lemon slices and sprigs of fresh parsley.

Sweet and Spicy Pacific Salmon Fillets

Prep time: 10 minutes | Cook time: 1½ hours | Serves 6

- 3 pounds (1.4 kg) salmon fillets
- ½ cup Colman's English mustard
- ¼ cup honey
- 2 tablespoons finely chopped fresh dill

1. Place the salmon in the insert of a 5- to 7-quart Ninja Foodi PossibleCooker. Put the mustard, honey, and dill in a small bowl and stir to combine. 2. Pour the mixture over the salmon, spreading evenly. 3. Cover and cook on high for 1½ hours, until the salmon is cooked through. 4. Serve the salmon from the Ninja Foodi PossibleCooker topped with some of the sauce.

Sea Bass Tagine

Prep time: 25 minutes | Cook time: 6 to 7½ hours | Serves 6

- 2 pounds (907 g) sea bass fillets
- ½ cup olive oil
- Grated zest of 1 lemon
- ¼ cup lemon juice
- 1 teaspoon sweet paprika
- ½ cup finely chopped fresh cilantro
- 2 cloves garlic, chopped
- 1 medium onion, finely chopped
- 1 teaspoon ground cumin
- ½ teaspoon saffron threads, crushed
- 1 (28- to 32-ounce / 794- to 907-g) can crushed tomatoes, with their juice
- 6 medium Yukon gold potatoes, quartered
- 1 teaspoon salt
- ½ teaspoon freshly ground black pepper
- ½ cup finely chopped fresh Italian parsley

1. Place the fish fillets into a resealable plastic bag. 2. In a small bowl, whisk together ¼ cup of the oil, lemon zest, lemon juice, paprika, and chopped cilantro. Pour this marinade over the fish in the bag, seal tightly, and refrigerate for at least 1 hour or up to 4 hours to let the flavors infuse. 3. Heat the remaining ¼ cup of oil in a large skillet over medium-high heat. Add the minced garlic, diced onion, ground cumin, and saffron, sautéing for 5 to 7 minutes or until the onion softens and becomes fragrant. 4. Stir in the diced tomatoes, mixing well. In the bottom of a 5- to 7-quart Ninja Foodi PossibleCooker insert, place the sliced potatoes and season them evenly with salt and black pepper, tossing to coat. Pour the tomato-onion mixture over the potatoes. Cover and cook on low for 5 to 6 hours, or until the potatoes are nearly tender. 5. Pour the reserved marinade into the Ninja Foodi PossibleCooker, stirring the potatoes and sauce to combine. Lay the marinated fish fillets on top of the potatoes, spooning some of the sauce over the fish. Cover and cook for an additional 1 to 1½ hours, or until the sea bass is opaque and cooked through. 6. Sprinkle chopped parsley over the top of the fish and serve immediately, ensuring to scoop up some potatoes and sauce alongside the fish.

Mediterranean Cod au Gratin

Prep time: 20 minutes | Cook time: 1 hour | Serves 6

- 6 tablespoons olive oil
- 3 tablespoons all-purpose flour
- 1½ teaspoons sea salt
- ½ tablespoon dry mustard
- 1 teaspoon rosemary
- ¼ tablespoon ground nutmeg
- 1¼ cups milk
- 2 teaspoons lemon juice
- ⅓ cup grated Parmesan cheese
- ⅓ cup grated Asiago cheese
- ⅓ cup grated Romano cheese
- 3 pounds (1.4 kg) Pacific cod fillets

Make the Orange Layer: 1. Warm the olive oil in a small saucepan over medium heat. Add the flour, salt, mustard, rosemary, and a dash of nutmeg, stirring until well blended. 2. Slowly pour in the milk, stirring constantly to avoid lumps, and continue cooking until the mixture thickens. 3. Stir in the lemon juice, followed by the Parmesan, Asiago, and Romano cheeses. Mix until the cheeses are fully melted and the sauce is smooth. 4. Arrange the fish in the Ninja Foodi PossibleCooker, then pour the cheese sauce evenly over the fish. Cover and cook on high for 1 to 1½ hours, or until the fish flakes easily with a fork. Serve hot.

Herb-Butter Garlic Tilapia Packets

Prep time: 5 minutes | Cook time: 2 hours | Serves 4

- 2 tablespoons butter, at room temperature
- 2 cloves garlic, minced
- 2 teaspoons minced fresh
- flat-leaf parsley
- 4 tilapia fillets
- Sea salt
- Black pepper

1. In a small bowl, mix the butter, garlic, and parsley to combine. 2. Pull out a large sheet of aluminum foil and put it on the counter. Place the fillets in the middle of the foil. 3. Season the fish generously with salt and pepper. 4. Evenly divide the butter mixture among the fillets and place on top. 5. Wrap the foil around the fish, sealing all sides and crimping the edges to make a packet. Place in the Ninja Foodi PossibleCooker, cover, and cook on high for 2 hours. Serve hot.

Spicy Tomato Basil Mussels

- 3 tablespoons olive oil
- 4 cloves garlic, minced
- 3 shallot cloves, minced
- 8 ounces (227 g) mushrooms, diced
- 1 (28-ounce / 794-g) can diced tomatoes, with the juice
- ¾ cup white wine
- 2 tablespoons dried oregano
- ½ tablespoon dried basil
- ½ teaspoon black pepper
- 1 teaspoon paprika
- ¼ teaspoon red pepper flakes
- 3 pounds (1.4 kg) mussels

1. Heat the olive oil in a large sauté pan over medium-high heat. Add the minced garlic, chopped shallots, and sliced mushrooms, cooking for 2 to 3 minutes until the garlic turns lightly golden and aromatic. Transfer everything from the pan into the Ninja Foodi PossibleCooker. 2. Pour in the tomatoes and white wine, then sprinkle with dried oregano, basil, black pepper, paprika, and a pinch of red pepper flakes. 3. Cover the Ninja Foodi PossibleCooker and let it cook on low for 4 to 5 hours, or on high for 2 to 3 hours, until the mushrooms are tender and flavorful. 4. While the mushroom mixture finishes, clean and debeard the mussels, discarding any that are already open. 5. Once the mushroom mixture is done, turn the heat setting on the Ninja Foodi PossibleCooker to high. Add the prepared mussels, secure the lid, and cook for another 30 minutes, or until the mussels have opened. 6. To serve, ladle the mussels and plenty of broth into bowls. Discard any mussels that remained closed. Serve hot with crusty bread to soak up the delicious broth.

Lemon, Garlic, and Butter Halibut

- 1 cup (2 sticks) unsalted butter
- ½ cup olive oil
- 6 cloves garlic, sliced
- 1 teaspoon sweet paprika
- ½ cup lemon juice
- Grated zest of 1 lemon
- ¼ cup finely chopped fresh chives
- 2 to 3 pounds (907 g to 1.4 kg) halibut fillets
- ½ cup finely chopped fresh Italian parsley

1. In the insert of a 5- to 7-quart Ninja Foodi PossibleCooker, combine the butter, oil, minced garlic, paprika, lemon juice, lemon zest, and chopped chives. Stir well to mix the ingredients thoroughly. Cover the Ninja Foodi PossibleCooker and set it to low, allowing the flavors to meld for 4 hours. 2. Carefully add the halibut fillets to the Ninja Foodi PossibleCooker, ensuring the sauce is spooned generously over the fish. Re-cover and continue cooking on low for an additional 40 minutes, or until the halibut is fully cooked and turns opaque. 3. Evenly sprinkle chopped parsley over the fish, and serve immediately while hot.

Spicy Coconut Seafood Laksa Noodle Soup

- 2 tablespoons virgin coconut oil or extra-virgin olive oil
- 1 small onion, chopped
- 4 Thai bird chiles
- 1 (2-inch) piece fresh ginger, peeled and grated
- 1 (1-inch) piece fresh turmeric, peeled and grated
- 1 lemongrass stalk, tough outer leaves discarded, inner bulb chopped
- ¼ cup fresh cilantro
- 1 tablespoon tamarind paste
- ½ teaspoon ground cumin
- ½ teaspoon paprika
- 2 teaspoon coarse salt
- 2 cups unsweetened coconut milk
- 2 cups boiling water
- 4 kaffir lime leaves
- 2 teaspoon fish sauce
- 1 pound (454 g) medium shrimp, peeled and deveined (shells rinsed and reserved)
- 2 pounds (907 g) small mussels, scrubbed
- ¾ pound (340 g) firm fish fillet, such as halibut or cod, cut into 1-inch pieces
- 8 ounces (227 g) rice noodles
- Lime wedges, cubed firm tofu, sliced scallions, sliced Thai bird chiles, cilantro, and chili oil, for serving

1. Preheat a 7-quart Ninja Foodi PossibleCooker. 2. Heat oil in a saucepan over medium. Add onion and cook until translucent, about 5 minutes. Add chiles, ginger, turmeric, lemongrass, cilantro, tamarind paste, cumin, paprika, and salt. Cook until fragrant, about 2 more minutes. Remove from heat and let cool. Transfer spice mixture to a food processor and puree to a thick paste. 3. Combine laksa paste, coconut milk, the boiling water, lime leaves, fish sauce, and shrimp shells in the Ninja Foodi PossibleCooker. Cover and cook on low for 2 hours (we prefer this recipe on low). 4. Strain liquid through a medium sieve into a bowl, pressing down on solids; return broth to Ninja Foodi PossibleCooker (discard solids). Add shrimp and mussels, and cook on low 20 minutes. Add fish and cook until shrimp is completely cooked through, fish is firm, and mussels open, about 10 minutes. 5. Meanwhile, prepare noodles according to package instructions. 6. To serve, divide noodles among bowls. Add broth and seafood, and top with tofu, scallions, chiles, and cilantro. Serve with lime wedges and chili oil.

Miso-Glazed Poached Salmon with Honey

Prep time: 10 minutes | Cook time: 1½ hours | Serves 8

- 3 pounds (1.4 kg) salmon fillets
- 3 tablespoons white miso
- 3 tablespoons honey
- ¼ cup rice wine (mirin) or dry sherry
- 2 teaspoons freshly grated ginger

1. place the salmon in the insert of a 5- to 7-quart Ninja Foodi PossibleCooker. 2. Combine the miso, honey, rice wine, and ginger in a mixing bowl and stir. 3. Pour the sauce over the salmon in the Ninja Foodi PossibleCooker. Cover and cook on high for 1½ hours, until the salmon is cooked through and registers 165°F (74°C) on an instant-read thermometer inserted in the center of a thick fillet. 4. Carefully remove the salmon from the slow-cooker insert with a large spatula. Remove the skin from the underside of the salmon (if necessary) and arrange the salmon on a serving platter. 5. Strain the sauce through a fine-mesh sieve into a saucepan. Boil the sauce, reduce it to a syrupy consistency, and serve with the salmon.

Potato-Crusted Sea Bass

Prep time: 15 minutes | Cook time: 1½ hours | Serves 6

- 1 cup (2 sticks) unsalted butter, melted and cooled
- ½ cup fresh lemon juice
- Grated zest of 1 lemon
- 2 cloves garlic, minced
- 8 tablespoons olive oil
- 2 tablespoons Old Bay

- seasoning
- 2 to 3 pounds (907 g to 1.4 kg) sea bass fillets, cut to fit the slow-cooker insert
- 6 medium Yukon gold potatoes, cut into ¼-inch-thick slices

1. In a small bowl, mix together the butter, lemon juice, lemon zest, minced garlic, and 2 tablespoons of olive oil. In a separate large bowl, combine the remaining 6 tablespoons of olive oil with the seasoning. 2. Brush the sea bass with a portion of the butter sauce and set it aside. Toss the potatoes in the bowl with the seasoned oil until well coated. Pour half of the butter sauce into the bottom of a 5- to 7-quart Ninja Foodi PossibleCooker. 3. Layer half of the seasoned potatoes in the bottom of the Ninja Foodi PossibleCooker.

Lay the sea bass over the potatoes and pour half of the remaining butter sauce over the fish. Add the remaining potatoes on top of the sea bass and drizzle with the rest of the butter sauce. 4. Cover and cook on high for 1½ hours, or until the potatoes start to turn golden and the sea bass is cooked through and opaque in the center. Remove the lid and cook for an additional 15 to 20 minutes to enhance the texture. 5. Serve immediately, ensuring each serving includes both sea bass and potatoes.

Bouillabaisse

Prep time: 25 minutes | Cook time: 7 to 9 hours | Serves 6 to 8

- ¼ cup extra-virgin olive oil
- 3 leeks, cleaned and coarsely chopped, using the white and tender green parts
- 4 cloves garlic, sliced
- 1 bulb fennel, ends trimmed, coarsely chopped
- Grated zest of 1 orange
- 1 teaspoon dried thyme
- 1 teaspoon saffron threads, crushed
- Pinch of cayenne pepper
- 1 (28- to 32-ounce / 794-

- to 907-g) can crushed tomatoes, with their juice
- ½ cup white wine or dry vermouth
- 3 cups clam juice
- 1 cup chicken broth
- ½ pound (227 g) littleneck clams
- ½ pound (227 g) mussels
- 3 pounds (1.4 kg) thick-fleshed fish, cut into 1-inch chunks
- ½ cup finely chopped fresh Italian parsley

1. Warm the oil in a large skillet over medium-high heat. Add the sliced leeks, minced garlic, fennel, citrus zest, thyme, saffron, and a pinch of cayenne. Sauté the mixture for around 2 minutes, or until the vegetables are tender. Stir in the diced tomatoes and wine, allowing it to simmer for 10 minutes to enhance the flavors. Transfer everything to the insert of a 5- to 7-quart Ninja Foodi PossibleCooker. 2. Pour in the clam juice and broth, stirring well to combine. Cover with the lid and cook on low for 6 to 8 hours. Once done, remove the lid and add the clams and mussels to the sauce. 3. Gently place the fish fillets on top of the shellfish, then ladle some sauce over the fish. Cover and switch to high heat, cooking for another 45 minutes, or until the fish is opaque and fully cooked, and the clams and mussels have opened. 4. Discard any shellfish that remain closed. Finish by sprinkling chopped parsley over the dish and serve immediately.

Sweet and Tangy Honey Glazed Salmon Fillets

Prep time: 10 minutes | Cook time: 1 hour | Serves 6

- 6 (6-ounce / 170-g) salmon fillets
- ½ cup honey
- 2 tablespoons lime juice
- 3 tablespoons
- Worcestershire sauce
- 1 tablespoon water
- 2 cloves garlic, minced
- 1 teaspoon ground ginger
- ½ teaspoon black pepper

1. Place the salmon fillets in the Ninja Foodi PossibleCooker. 2. In medium bowl, whisk the honey, lime juice, Worcestershire sauce, water, garlic, ginger, and pepper. Pour sauce over salmon. 3. Cover and cook on high for 1 hour.

Mahi-Mahi with Pineapple-Mango-Strawberry Salsa and Lentils

Prep time: 30 minutes | Cook time: 6 hours | Serves 6

- 1¼ cups vegetable or chicken stock
- 1 cup orange juice
- ¾ cup orange lentils
- ½ cup finely diced carrot
- ¼ cup finely diced red onion
- ¼ cup finely diced celery

Salsa:
- ¾ cup finely diced pineapple
- ¾ cup finely diced mango
- ½ cup finely diced strawberries
- ¼ cup finely diced red onion

- 1 tablespoon honey
- 6 (4- to-5-ounce / 113- to 142-g) mahi-mahi fillets
- Sea salt
- Black pepper
- 1 teaspoon lemon juice

- 2 tablespoons chopped fresh mint (or 2 teaspoons dried)
- 2 tablespoons orange juice
- 1 tablespoon lime juice
- ¼ teaspoon salt

1. In the Ninja Foodi PossibleCooker, add the stock, orange juice, lentils, diced carrot, chopped onion, celery pieces, and honey. Mix everything thoroughly. 2. Secure the lid and let it cook on the low setting for 5 to 5½ hours, or until the lentils become tender. 3. Lay a piece of parchment paper directly over the lentils in the Ninja Foodi PossibleCooker. Lightly season the mahi-mahi with salt and black pepper, and place it skin-side down on the parchment if the skin hasn't been removed. Cover the Ninja Foodi PossibleCooker again and continue cooking on low for another 25 minutes, or until the fish turns opaque in the middle. Carefully remove the fish by lifting the parchment paper and set it on a plate. 4. Add the lemon juice to the cooked lentils and adjust seasoning with salt and black pepper. To prepare the Salsa: 5. As the mahi-mahi finishes cooking, mix the pineapple, mango, strawberries, finely diced red onion, chopped fresh mint, orange juice, lime juice, and a pinch of salt in a large jar. Shake well and refrigerate so the flavors can meld. 6. When serving, spoon about ½ cup of warm lentils onto a plate, place a mahi-mahi fillet on top, and finish with about ⅓ cup of chilled fruit salsa.

Acadiana Shrimp Barbecue

Prep time: 15 minutes | Cook time: 4 hours | Serves 6 to 8

- 1 cup (2 sticks) unsalted butter
- ¼ cup olive oil
- 8 cloves garlic, sliced
- 2 teaspoons dried oregano
- 1 teaspoon dried thyme
- ½ teaspoon freshly ground black pepper

- Pinch of cayenne pepper
- 2 teaspoons sweet paprika
- ¼ cup Worcestershire sauce
- ¼ cup lemon juice
- 3 pounds (1.4 kg) large shrimp, peeled and deveined
- ½ cup finely chopped fresh Italian parsley

1. Add the butter, oil, minced garlic, dried oregano, thyme, black pepper, cayenne, paprika, Worcestershire sauce, and lemon juice to the insert of a 5- to 7-quart Ninja Foodi PossibleCooker. Cover and let it cook on low for 4 hours to allow the flavors to blend. 2. Increase the heat to high and add the shrimp, stirring to coat them evenly in the flavorful butter sauce. Cover and cook for 10 to 15 minutes, or until the shrimp turn pink and are cooked through. 3. Remove the shrimp from the Ninja Foodi PossibleCooker and place them in a large serving bowl. Pour the rich sauce over the shrimp and garnish with chopped parsley. Serve immediately.

Saffron-Infused Catalan Seafood Stew

Prep time: 20 minutes | Cook time: 7 hours | Serves 6 to 8

- ½ cup extra-virgin olive oil
- 2 medium onions, finely chopped
- 2 medium red bell peppers, seeded and finely chopped
- 6 cloves garlic, minced
- 1 teaspoon saffron threads, crushed
- 1 teaspoon hot paprika
- 1 cup finely chopped Spanish chorizo or soppressata salami
- 1 (28- to 32-ounce / 794- to 907-g) can crushed tomatoes
- 2 cups clam juice
- 1 cup chicken broth
- 2 pounds (907 g) firm-fleshed fish, such as halibut, monkfish, cod, or sea bass fillets, cut into 1-inch chunks
- 1½ pounds (680 g) littleneck clams
- ½ cup finely chopped fresh Italian parsley

1. Heat the oil in a large skillet over medium-high heat. Add the onions, bell peppers, garlic, saffron, paprika, and chorizo and sauté until the vegetables are softened, 5 to 7 minutes. Add the tomatoes and transfer the contents of the skillet to the insert of a 5- to 7-quart Ninja Foodi PossibleCooker. Add the clam juice and broth and stir to combine. 2. Cover and cook on low for 6 hours. Add the fish and clams to the slow-cooker insert, spooning some of the sauce over the fish and pushing the clams under the sauce. 3. Cover and cook for an additional 45 to 50 minutes, until the clams have opened and the fish is cooked through and opaque. Discard any clams that haven't opened. 4. Sprinkle the parsley over the stew and serve immediately.

Cajun Shrimp

Prep time: 15 minutes | Cook time: 3½ to 7 hours | Serves 6

- ¾ pound (340 g) andouille sausage, cut into ½-inch rounds (you may substitute Kiel-basa if you cannot find andouille sausage)
- 1 red onion, sliced into wedges
- 2 garlic cloves, minced
- 2 celery stalks, coarsely chopped
- 1 red or green bell pepper, coarsely chopped
- 2 tablespoons all-purpose flour
- 1 (28-ounce / 794-g) can diced tomatoes, with their juice
- ¼ teaspoon cayenne pepper
- Coarse sea salt
- ½ pound (227 g) large shrimp, peeled and deveined
- 2 cups fresh okra, sliced (you may substitute frozen and thawed, if necessary)

1. Place the sausage, chopped onion, minced garlic, diced celery, and bell pepper into the Ninja Foodi PossibleCooker. Sprinkle the flour over the mixture and toss well to evenly coat everything. 2. Pour in the diced tomatoes and ½ cup of water. Season with cayenne pepper and a pinch of salt, mixing everything to combine. 3. Cover the Ninja Foodi PossibleCooker and cook on high for 3½ hours or on low for 7 hours, until the vegetables are soft and flavorful. 4. Add the shrimp and sliced okra to the Ninja Foodi PossibleCooker. Cover again and continue cooking until the shrimp are fully cooked and opaque, about 30 minutes on high or 1 hour on low. Serve hot and enjoy.

Chapter

7

Snacks and Appetizers

Chapter 7 Snacks and Appetizers

Savory Pizza Dip with Herbs and Garlic

Prep time: 15 minutes	Cook time: 3 to 4 hours	Serves 8

- 2 tablespoons extra-virgin olive oil
- 1 medium onion, finely chopped
- 2 teaspoons dried oregano
- 2 teaspoons dried basil
- Pinch of red pepper flakes
- 3 cloves garlic, minced
- 2 (14- to 15-ounce / 397- to 425-g) cans crushed plum tomatoes, with their juice
- 2 tablespoons tomato paste
- 1 ½ teaspoons salt
- ½ teaspoon freshly ground black pepper
- ½ cup finely chopped fresh Italian parsley

1. Heat the oil in a small saucepan over medium-high heat. Add the onion, oregano, basil, red pepper flakes, and garlic and sauté until the onion is softened, about 3 minutes. 2. Transfer the contents of the skillet to the insert of a 1½- to 3-quart Ninja Foodi PossibleCooker. Add the remaining ingredients and stir to combine. Cover and cook on low for 3 to 4 hours. 3. Serve from the cooker set on warm.

Slim Dunk

Prep time: 10 minutes	Cook time: 1 hour	Serves 12

- 2 cups fat-free sour cream
- ¼ cup fat-free miracle whip salad dressing
- 1 (10-ounce / 283-g) package frozen chopped spinach, squeezed dry and chopped
- 1 (1.8-ounce / 51-g) envelope dry leek soup mix
- ¼ cup red bell pepper, minced

1. Place all the ingredients into the Ninja Foodi PossibleCooker and stir thoroughly to ensure everything is well mixed. 2. Cover the Ninja Foodi PossibleCooker and set it to high, cooking for 1 hour until flavors are well combined and the dish is heated through. 3. Serve hot and enjoy immediately.

Cheesy Loaded Veggie Dip with Spinach and Herbs

Prep time: 1 hour	Cook time: 1 hour	Makes 5 cups

- ¾ cup finely chopped fresh broccoli
- ½ cup finely chopped cauliflower
- ½ cup finely chopped fresh carrot
- ½ cup finely chopped red onion
- ½ cup finely chopped celery
- 2 garlic cloves, minced
- 4 tablespoons olive oil, divided
- 1 (14-ounce / 397-g) can water-packed artichoke hearts, rinsed, drained and chopped
- 1 (6½-ounce / 184-g) package spreadable garlic and herb cream cheese
- 1 (1.4-ounce / 40-g) package vegetable recipe mix (Knorr)
- 1 teaspoon garlic powder
- ½ teaspoon white pepper
- ⅛ to ¼ teaspoon cayenne pepper
- ¼ cup vegetable broth
- ¼ cup half-and-half cream
- 3 cups shredded Italian cheese blend
- ½ cup minced fresh basil
- 1 (9-ounce / 255-g) package fresh spinach, finely chopped
- Assorted crackers or baked pita chips

1. In a large skillet, saute the broccoli, cauliflower, carrot, onion, celery and garlic in 2 tablespoons oil until tender. Stir in the artichokes, cream cheese, vegetable recipe mix, garlic powder, white pepper and cayenne; set aside. 2. In a 3-quart Ninja Foodi PossibleCooker, combine broth, cream and remaining oil. Stir in broccoli mixture, Italian cheese blend and basil. Fold in spinach. Cover and cook on low for 1 to 2 hours or until cheese is melted and spinach is tender. Serve with crackers.

Curried Almonds

Prep time: 5 minutes | Cook time: 3 to 4½ hours | Makes 4 cups nuts

- 2 tablespoons butter, melted
- 1 tablespoon curry powder
- ½ teaspoon seasoned salt
- 1 pound (454 g) blanched almonds

1. Mix the melted butter with curry powder and seasoned salt in a small bowl. 2. Pour the seasoned butter over the almonds in the Ninja Foodi PossibleCooker, stirring to ensure the almonds are evenly coated. 3. Cover the Ninja Foodi PossibleCooker and cook on low for 2 to 3 hours. Then, switch to high, uncover, and continue cooking for an additional 1 to 1½ hours, stirring occasionally. 4. Serve the almonds either hot or cold, depending on your preference.

Snack Mix

Prep time: 10 minutes | Cook time: 2 hours | Serves 10 to 14

- 8 cups Chex cereal, of any combination
- 6 cups pretzels
- 6 tablespoons butter, melted
- 2 tablespoons
- Worcestershire sauce
- 1 teaspoon seasoned salt
- ½ teaspoon garlic powder
- ½ teaspoon onion salt
- ½ teaspoon onion powder

1. Place the first two ingredients into the Ninja Foodi PossibleCooker and mix together. 2. Melt the butter and combine it with the seasonings. Pour the butter mixture over the dry ingredients, tossing until everything is evenly coated. 3. Cover the Ninja Foodi PossibleCooker and cook on low for 2 hours, stirring every 30 minutes to ensure even cooking and flavor distribution.

Decadent Chocolate Peanut Clusters

Prep time: 20 minutes | Cook time: 3 hours | Makes 3½ to 4 dozen pieces

- 2 pounds (907 g) white candy coating, chopped
- 1 (12-ounce / 340-g) package semi-sweet chocolate chips
- 1 (4-ounce / 113-g) milk
- chocolate bar, or 1 (4-ounce / 113-g) package German sweet chocolate, chopped
- 1 (24-ounce / 680-g) jar dry roasted peanuts
- Nonstick cooking spray

1. Spray inside of Ninja Foodi PossibleCooker with nonstick cooking spray. 2. In Ninja Foodi PossibleCooker, combine white candy coating, chocolate chips, and milk chocolate. 3. Cover and cook on low 3 hours. Stir every 15 minutes. 4. Add peanuts to melted chocolate. Mix well. 5. Drop by tablespoonfuls onto waxed paper. Cool until set. Serve immediately, or store in a tightly covered container, separating layers with waxed paper. Keep cool and dry.

Hearty Beef Dip Fondue

Prep time: 20 minutes | Cook time: 6 hours | Makes 2½ cups

- 1¾ cups milk
- 2 (8-ounce / 227-g) packages cream cheese, cubed
- 2 teaspoons dry mustard
- ¼ cup chopped green onions
- 2½ ounces (71 g) sliced dried beef, shredded or torn into small pieces
- French bread, cut into bite-sized pieces, each having a side of crust

1. Pour the milk into the Ninja Foodi PossibleCooker and heat on high until warmed through. 2. Gradually add the cheese, stirring continuously until it is fully melted and smooth. 3. Mix in the mustard, chopped green onions, and diced dried beef, stirring well to combine. 4. Cover the Ninja Foodi PossibleCooker and set it to low, cooking for up to 6 hours to keep the mixture warm and flavorful. 5. Serve hot, using long forks to dip pieces of bread into the cheesy mixture.

Creamy Warm Clam and Herb Dip

Prep time: 15 minutes | Cook time: 2 to 3 hours | Serves 6 to 8

- 2 (8-ounce / 227-g) packages cream cheese at room temperature and cut into cubes
- ½ cup mayonnaise
- 3 green onions, finely chopped, using the white and tender green parts
- 2 cloves garlic, minced
- 3 (8-ounce / 227-g) cans minced or chopped clams, drained with ¼ cup clam juice reserved
- 1 tablespoon Worcestershire sauce
- 2 teaspoons anchovy paste
- ¼ cup finely chopped fresh Italian parsley

1. Coat the insert of a 1½- to 3-quart Ninja Foodi PossibleCooker with nonstick cooking spray. Combine all the ingredients in a large mixing bowl, adding the clam juice to thin the dip. 2. Transfer the mixture to the Ninja Foodi PossibleCooker, cover, and cook on low for 2 to 3 hours, until bubbling. 3. Serve from the cooker set on warm.

Creamy Mornay Dip for Crab and Shrimp

Prep time: 10 minutes | Cook time: 2 to 3 hours | Serves 8

- 2 tablespoons unsalted butter
- 2 medium shallots, finely chopped
- 2 teaspoons Old Bay seasoning
- 2 tablespoons all-purpose flour
- 2 cups lobster stock
- ¼ cup cream sherry
- 1 cup heavy cream
- ¼ cup finely chopped fresh Italian parsley

1. Melt the butter in a small saucepan over medium-high heat. Add the shallots and seasoning and cook for 2 minutes, until the shallots are softened. Add the flour and cook for 3 minutes, whisking constantly. Gradually whisk in the stock and sherry and bring the mixture to a boil. 2. Stir in the cream and parsley to combine. Transfer to the insert of a 1½- to 3-quart Ninja Foodi PossibleCooker. Cover and cook on low for 2 to 3 hours. 3. Serve from the cooker set on warm.

Sweet and Tangy Barbecued Little Smokies

Prep time: 5 minutes | Cook time: 4 hours | Serves 48 to 60 as an appetizer

- 4 (16-ounce / 454-g) packages little smokies
- 1 (18-ounce / 510-g) bottle barbecue sauce

1. Mix ingredients together in Ninja Foodi PossibleCooker. 2. Cover and cook on low for 4 hours.
"Baked" Brie with Cranberry Chutney
Prep time: 10 minutes | Cook time: 4 hours | Serves 8 to 10

- 1 cup fresh or dried cranberries
- ½ cup brown sugar
- ⅓ cup cider vinegar
- 2 tablespoons water or orange juice
- 2 teaspoons minced crystallized ginger
- ¼ teaspoon cinnamon
- ⅛ teaspoon ground cloves
- Oil
- 1 (8-ounce / 227-g) round of Brie cheese
- 1 tablespoon sliced almonds, toasted
- Crackers

1. In the Ninja Foodi PossibleCooker, mix together the cranberries, brown sugar, vinegar, water or juice, grated ginger, cinnamon, and cloves until well combined. 2. Cover and cook on low for 4 hours, stirring once near the end to check if the mixture is thickening. If it hasn't thickened, remove the lid, turn the heat to high, and cook for an additional 30 minutes without the lid. 3. Transfer the cranberry chutney to a covered container and refrigerate for up to 2 weeks. When ready to serve, let it come to room temperature. 4. Lightly brush an ovenproof plate with oil, place the unpeeled Brie on the plate, and bake uncovered at 350ºF (180ºC) for 9 minutes, or until the cheese is soft and partially melted. Remove from the oven. 5. Spoon at least half of the cranberry chutney over the Brie and sprinkle with sliced almonds. Serve immediately with crackers.

Liver Paté

Prep time: 15 minutes | Cook time: 4 to 5 hours | Makes 1½ cups paté

- 1 pound (454 g) chicken livers
- ½ cup dry wine
- 1 teaspoon instant chicken bouillon
- 1 teaspoon minced parsley
- 1 tablespoon instant minced onion
- ¼ teaspoon ground ginger
- ½ teaspoon seasoned salt
- 1 tablespoon soy sauce
- ¼ teaspoon dry mustard
- ¼ cup soft butter
- 1 tablespoon brandy

1. Combine all the ingredients, except for the butter and brandy, in the Ninja Foodi PossibleCooker. 2. Cover and cook on low for 4 to 5 hours. Allow the mixture to stand in the liquid until it has cooled. 3. Drain the cooled mixture and transfer it to a blender or food grinder. Add the butter and brandy, then blend until smooth and creamy. 4. Serve immediately or store for later use.

Creamy Buffalo Chicken Wing Dip

Prep time: 20 minutes | Cook time: 2 hours | Makes 6 cups

- 2 (8-ounce / 227-g) packages cream cheese, softened
- ½ cup ranch salad dressing
- ½ cup sour cream
- 5 tablespoons crumbled blue cheese
- 2 cups shredded cooked chicken
- ½ cup Buffalo wing sauce
- 2 cups shredded cheddar cheese, divided
- 1 green onion, sliced
- Tortilla chips

1. In a small bowl, combine the cream cheese, dressing, sour cream and blue cheese. Transfer to a 3-quart Ninja Foodi PossibleCooker. Layer with chicken, wing sauce and 1 cup cheese. Cover and cook on low for 2 to 3 hours or until heated through. 2. Sprinkle with remaining cheese and onion. Serve with tortilla chips.

Creamy Reuben Cheese Spread

Prep time: 10 minutes | Cook time: 4 hours | Serves 3

- 2 (8-ounce / 227-g) packages cream cheese, cubed
- 4 cups shredded Swiss cheese
- 1 (14-ounce / 397-g) can sauerkraut, rinsed and well drained
- 4 (2-ounce / 57-g) packages thinly sliced deli corned beef, chopped
- ½ cup Thousand Island salad dressing
- Snack rye bread or rye crackers

1. Place the first five ingredients in a 1½-quart Ninja Foodi PossibleCooker; stir to combine. Cook, covered, on low 4 to 4½ hours or until heated through. 2. Stir to blend. Serve spread with bread.

Mini Hot Dogs and Meatballs

Prep time: 5 minutes | Cook time: 2 to 3 hours | Serves 15

- 36 frozen cooked Italian meatballs (½-ounce / 14-g each)
- 1 (16-ounce / 454-g) package miniature hot dogs or little smoked sausages
- 1 (26-ounce / 737-g) jar meatless spaghetti sauce
- 1 (18-ounce / 510-g) bottle barbecue sauce
- 1 (12-ounce / 340-g) bottle chili sauce

1. Place all the ingredients into the Ninja Foodi PossibleCooker and mix well to combine. 2. Cover and cook on high for 2 hours or on low for 3 hours, until everything is heated through and flavors have melded.

Lemon Butter Steamed Artichokes

Prep time: 10 minutes | Cook time: 2½ to 4 hours | Serves 4

- 4 whole, fresh artichokes
- 1 teaspoon salt
- 4 tablespoons lemon juice, divided
- 2 tablespoons butter, melted

1. Wash and trim off the tough outer leaves and around the bottom of the artichokes. Cut off about 1 inch from the tops of each, and trim off the tips of the leaves. Spread the top leaves apart and use a long-handled spoon to pull out the fuzzy chokes in their centers. 2. Stand the prepared artichokes upright in the Ninja Foodi PossibleCooker. Sprinkle each with ¼ teaspoon salt. 3. Spoon 2 tablespoons lemon juice over the artichokes. Pour in enough water to cover the bottom half of the artichokes. 4. Cover and cook on high for 2½ to 4 hours. 5. Serve with melted butter and remaining lemon juice for dipping.

Bacon-Pineapple Tater Tot Bake

Prep time: 15 minutes | Cook time: 4 hours | Serves 8

- 1 (32-ounce / 907-g) package frozen tater tots, thawed
- 8 ounces (227 g) Canadian bacon, chopped
- 1 cup frozen pepper strips, thawed and chopped
- 1 medium onion, finely chopped
- 1 (8-ounce / 227-g) can pineapple tidbits, drained
- 2 eggs
- 3 (5-ounce / 142-g) cans evaporated milk
- 1 (15-ounce / 425-g) can pizza sauce
- 1 cup shredded provolone cheese
- ½ cup grated Parmesan cheese (optional)

1. Grease a 5-quart Ninja Foodi PossibleCooker and layer half of the Tater Tots in the bottom. Add a layer of Canadian bacon, diced peppers, chopped onion, and pineapple chunks. Top with the remaining Tater Tots. In a large bowl, whisk together the eggs, milk, and pizza sauce until well blended, then pour the mixture evenly over the Tater Tot layers. Sprinkle with provolone cheese. 2. Cover and cook on low for 4 to 5 hours, or until the dish is fully heated and set. If desired, sprinkle with Parmesan cheese, cover again, and let stand for 20 minutes before serving.

Garlic Swiss Fondue

Prep time: 10 minutes | Cook time: 2 hours | Makes 3 cups

- 4 cups shredded Swiss cheese
- 1 (10¾-ounce / 305-g) can condensed cheddar cheese soup, undiluted
- 2 tablespoons sherry or chicken broth
- 1 tablespoon Dijon mustard
- 2 garlic cloves, minced
- 2 teaspoons hot pepper sauce
- Cubed French bread baguette
- Sliced apples
- Seedless red grapes

1. In a 1½-quart Ninja Foodi PossibleCooker, combine the first six ingredients, stirring to mix thoroughly. Cover and cook on low for 2 to 2½ hours, stirring every 30 minutes until the cheese is completely melted and smooth. 2. Serve warm, accompanied by bread cubes and fresh fruit for dipping.

Spicy Crocked Nuts

Prep time: 15 minutes | Cook time: 2 to 2½ hours | Serves 8

- 4 tablespoons (½ stick) unsalted butter, melted
- 2 teaspoons Lawry's seasoned salt
- 1 teaspoon garlic salt
- ⅛ teaspoon cayenne pepper
- 4 tablespoons sugar
- 4 cups pecan halves, walnut halves, or whole almonds

1. Place the butter, seasoned salt, garlic salt, cayenne pepper, and 2 tablespoons of sugar into the insert of a 5- to 7-quart Ninja Foodi PossibleCooker. Cover and cook on high for 20 minutes, until the butter is melted and the spices are well mixed. 2. Add the nuts to the Ninja Foodi PossibleCooker, stirring thoroughly to coat them in the buttery spice mixture. Cook uncovered on low for 2 to 2½ hours, stirring occasionally to ensure even cooking. 3. Sprinkle the remaining 2 tablespoons of sugar over the nuts and toss well to coat. Transfer the nuts to a baking sheet and let them cool completely before serving.

Creamy Southwestern Chili Queso Dip

Prep time: 20 minutes | Cook time: 2 to 3 hours | Serves 8

- 1 (8-ounce / 227-g) package cream cheese, cut into cubes
- 2 tablespoons unsalted butter
- 1 medium sweet onion, such as Vidalia, finely chopped
- 4 chipotle chiles in adobo, minced
- 1 medium red bell pepper, seeded and finely chopped
- 1 medium yellow bell pepper, seeded and finely chopped
- 2 teaspoons ground cumin
- 2 cups finely shredded sharp Cheddar cheese
- 2 cups finely shredded Monterey Jack cheese
- Fresh vegetables for serving
- Tortilla chips for serving

1. Coat the insert of a 1½- to 3-quart Ninja Foodi PossibleCooker with nonstick cooking spray. Turn the machine on low and add the cream cheese. Cover and let stand while preparing the other ingredients. 2. Melt the butter in a large sauté pan over medium-high heat. Add the onion, chipotles, bell peppers, and cumin and sauté until the bell peppers become softened, 4 to 5 minutes. Transfer the contents of the sauté pan into the slow-cooker insert and stir to blend with the cream cheese. 3. Fold in the Cheddar and Jack cheeses. Cover and cook on low for 2 to 3 hours. 4. Serve from the cooker set on warm with fresh vegetables and sturdy tortilla chips.

Hot Broccoli Dip

Prep time: 20 minutes | Cook time: 1 hour | Serves 24

- 2 cups fresh or frozen broccoli, chopped
- 4 tablespoons chopped red bell pepper
- 2 (8-ounce / 227-g)
- containers ranch dip
- ½ cup grated Parmesan cheese
- 2 cups shredded Cheddar cheese

1. Combine all the ingredients in your Ninja Foodi PossibleCooker, stirring to ensure everything is evenly mixed. 2. Cover and cook on low for 1 hour, or until heated through and flavors have melded. 3. Serve warm and enjoy.

Quick and Easy Barbecue Little Smokies

Prep time: 5 minutes | Cook time: 2 hours | Serves 12 to 16

- 1 (18-ounce / 510-g) bottle barbecue sauce
- 8 ounces (227 g) salsa
- 2 (16-ounce / 454-g) packages little smokies

1. Mix barbecue sauce and salsa in Ninja Foodi PossibleCooker. 2. Add the little smokies. 3. Heat on high for 2 hours. 4. Stir. Turn to low to serve.

Apple Kielbasa

Prep time: 15 minutes | Cook time: 6 to 8 hours | Serves 12

- 2 pounds (907 g) fully cooked kielbasa sausage, cut into 1-inch pieces
- ¾ cup brown sugar
- 1 cup chunky applesauce
- 2 cloves garlic, minced

1. Place all the ingredients into the Ninja Foodi PossibleCooker and mix well to combine. 2. Cover and cook on low for 6 to 8 hours, or until the dish is thoroughly heated and flavors have melded together.

Sweet and Savory Mini Hot Dogs

Prep time: 5 minutes | Cook time: 4 to 5 hours | Serves 20 to 30 as an appetizer

- 2 cups brown sugar
- 1 tablespoon Worcestershire sauce
- 1 (14-ounce / 397-g) bottle ketchup
- 2 or 3 pounds (907 g or 1.4 kg) mini-hot dogs

1. In Ninja Foodi PossibleCooker, mix together brown sugar, 2. Worcestershire sauce, and ketchup. Stir in hot dogs. 3. Cover and cook on high 1 hour. Turn to low and cook 3 to 4 hours. 4. Serve from the cooker while turned to low.

Chili Nuts

Prep time: 5 minutes | Cook time: 2 to 2½ hours | Makes 5 cups nuts

- ¼ cup butter, melted
- 2 (12-ounce / 340-g) cans cocktail peanuts
- 1 (1.6-ounce / 45-g) package chili seasoning mix

1. Pour the melted butter over the nuts in the Ninja Foodi PossibleCooker, ensuring they are evenly coated. 2. Sprinkle the dry chili mix over the nuts and toss well to combine. Cover and heat on low for 2 to 2½ hours. Then, turn the heat to high, remove the lid, and cook for an additional 10 to 15 minutes, stirring occasionally. 3. Serve the nuts warm or let them cool before serving.

Savory All-American Snack Mix

Prep time: 10 minutes | Cook time: 3 hours | Makes 3 quarts snack mix

- 3 cups thin pretzel sticks
- 4 cups Wheat Chex
- 4 cups Cheerios
- 1 (12-ounce / 340-g) can salted peanuts
- ¼ cup butter, melted
- 1 teaspoon garlic powder
- 1 teaspoon celery salt
- ½ teaspoon seasoned salt
- 2 tablespoons grated Parmesan cheese

1. Combine pretzels, cereal, and peanuts in large bowl. 2. Melt butter. Stir in garlic powder, celery salt, seasoned salt, and Parmesan cheese. Pour over pretzels and cereal. Toss until well mixed. 3. Pour into large Ninja Foodi PossibleCooker. Cover. Cook on low 2½ hours, stirring every 30 minutes. Remove lid and cook another 30 minutes on low. 4. Serve warm or at room temperature. Store in tightly covered container.

Maytag Blue and Walnut Dip with Apple Dippers

Prep time: 10 minutes | Cook time: 2 to 3 hours | Serves 8

- 2 (8-ounce / 227-g) packages cream cheese at room temperature
- ½ cup mayonnaise
- 2 tablespoons Ruby Port
- 6 drops Tabasco sauce
- 1 cup chopped walnuts
- 2 cups crumbled Maytag blue cheese
- 4 to 6 Granny Smith Apples, cored and cut into 8 wedges each, for serving
- Crackers for serving

1. Spray the insert of a 1½- to 3-quart Ninja Foodi PossibleCooker with nonstick cooking spray. In a mixing bowl, combine the cream cheese, mayonnaise, port, Tabasco sauce, chopped walnuts, and blue cheese, stirring until everything is evenly blended. 2. Spoon the mixture into the prepared slow-cooker insert. Cover and cook on low for 2 to 3 hours, or until the dip is thoroughly heated and bubbling. 3. Keep the Ninja Foodi PossibleCooker on the warm setting and serve the dip with apple wedges and crackers.

Spicy Barbecue Kielbasa with Bourbon Sauce

Prep time: 20 minutes | Cook time: 4 to 5 hours | Serves 8

- 2 cups ketchup
- ½ cup firmly packed light brown sugar
- 1 tablespoon Worcestershire sauce
- 1 teaspoon Creole mustard
- 1 teaspoon hot sauce
- 1 medium onion, finely chopped
- ½ cup bourbon
- 2 pounds (907 g) kielbasa or other smoked sausages, cut into ½-inch rounds

1. Combine all the ingredients in the insert of a 3- to 5-quart Ninja Foodi PossibleCooker. Cover and cook on low for 4 to 5 hours, until the sausage is heated through. 2. Serve the kielbasa from the cooker set on warm, with 6-inch skewers.

Chapter 8

Vegetables and Sides

Chapter 8 Vegetables and Sides

Rich Wild Mushroom Stroganoff

Prep time: 15 minutes | Cook time: 6 hours | Serves 6

- 3 tablespoons extra-virgin olive oil, divided
- 2 tablespoons butter
- 14 ounces (397 g) mushrooms, sliced
- ½ sweet onion, diced
- 2 teaspoons minced garlic
- 2 cups beef broth
- 3 tablespoons paprika
- 1 tablespoon tomato paste
- ½ cup heavy (whipping) cream
- ½ cup sour cream
- 2 tablespoons chopped parsley, for garnish

1. Lightly grease the insert of the Ninja Foodi PossibleCooker with 1 tablespoon of the olive oil. 2. In a large skillet over medium heat, heat the remaining 2 tablespoons of the olive oil and the butter. Add the mushrooms, onion, and garlic and sauté until they are softened, about 5 minutes. 3. Transfer the mushroom mixture to the insert and add the broth, paprika, and tomato paste. 4. Cover and cook on low for 6 hours. 5. Stir in the heavy cream and sour cream 6. Serve topped with the parsley.

Company Mashed Potatoes

Prep time: 20 minutes | Cook time: 12 to 16 hours | Serves 12

- 15 medium potatoes
- 1 cup sour cream
- 1 small onion, diced fine
- 1 teaspoon salt
- ⅛ to ¼ teaspoon pepper, according to your taste
- preference
- 1 to 2 cups buttermilk
- 1 cup fresh, chopped spinach (optional)
- 1 cup shredded Colby or Cheddar cheese (optional)

1. Peel and quarter the potatoes, then place them in the Ninja Foodi PossibleCooker. Add just enough water to barely cover the potatoes.

2. Cover and cook on low for 8 to 10 hours, until the potatoes are tender. Drain off the water. 3. Mash the potatoes directly in the Ninja Foodi PossibleCooker, then add the remaining ingredients, except for the cheese, mixing until well combined. 4. Cover and heat on low for an additional 4 to 6 hours. 5. Sprinkle the cheese over the potatoes about 5 minutes before serving, allowing it to melt. Serve warm.

Decadent Cheddar and Cream Cheese Mashed Potatoes

Prep time: 20 minutes | Cook time: 3 to 4 hours | Serves 8

- 8 large russet potatoes, peeled and cut into 1-inch chunks
- 4 tablespoons (½ stick) unsalted butter
- 1 cup finely shredded mild Cheddar cheese
- 1 (8-ounce / 227-g) package cream cheese at room
- temperature
- 1 cup sour cream
- 4 green onions, finely chopped, using the white and tender green parts
- 8 strips bacon, cooked crisp, drained, and crumbled
- Salt and freshly ground black pepper

1. Coat the insert of a 5- to 7-quart Ninja Foodi PossibleCooker with nonstick cooking spray or line with a slow-cooker liner according to the manufacturer's directions. 2. Cook the potatoes in salted water to cover until tender when pierced with the tip of a sharp knife. Drain the potatoes thoroughly and place in the bowl of an electric mixer. 3. Add 2 tablespoons of the butter, ½ cup of the Cheddar, the cream cheese, and sour cream and beat until fluffy and light. Stir in the green onions and bacon and season with salt and pepper. Transfer the potato mixture to the slow-cooker insert and top with the remaining butter and cheese. 4. Cover and cook on low for 3 to 4 hours, until the butter is melted and the potatoes are heated through. 5. Serve the potatoes from the cooker set on warm.

Sweet and Savory Stewed Tomatoes with Buttered Bread Crust

Prep time: 10 minutes | Cook time: 3 to 4 hours | Serves 12

- 2 quarts low-sodium canned tomatoes
- ¼ cup sugar
- 1 teaspoon salt
- Dash of black pepper
- 2 tablespoons butter
- 2 cups bread cubes

1. Place tomatoes in Ninja Foodi PossibleCooker. 2. Sprinkle with sugar, salt, and pepper. 3. Lightly toast bread cubes in melted butter in skillet on top of stove. Spread over tomatoes. 4. Cover. Cook on high 3 to 4 hours.

Very Special Spinach

Prep time: 10 minutes | Cook time: 5 hours | Serves 8

- 3 (10-ounce / 283-g) boxes frozen spinach, thawed and drained
- 2 cups cottage cheese
- 1½ cups shredded Cheddar cheese
- 3 eggs
- ¼ cup flour
- 1 teaspoon salt
- ½ cup butter, or margarine, melted

1. Combine all the ingredients in a large mixing bowl, stirring until well mixed. 2. Pour the mixture into the Ninja Foodi PossibleCooker, spreading it evenly. 3. Cook on high for 1 hour, then reduce the heat to low and continue cooking for an additional 4 hours, or until fully cooked and flavors have developed.

Hearty Bacon and Green Beans with Potatoes

Prep time: 15 minutes | Cook time: 6 hours | Serves 10

- 8 bacon strips, chopped
- 1½ pounds (680 g) fresh green beans, trimmed and cut into 2-inch pieces (about 4 cups)
- 4 medium potatoes, peeled and cubed (½ inch)
- 1 small onion, halved and sliced
- ¼ cup reduced-sodium chicken broth
- ½ teaspoon salt
- ¼ teaspoon pepper

1. In a large skillet, cook bacon over medium heat until crisp, stirring occasionally. Remove to paper towels with a slotted spoon; drain, reserving 1 tablespoon drippings. Cover and refrigerate bacon until serving. 2. In a 5-quart Ninja Foodi PossibleCooker, combine the remaining ingredients; stir in reserved drippings. Cover and cook on low for 6 to 8 hours or until potatoes are tender. Stir in bacon; heat through.

Pizza Potatoes

Prep time: 15 minutes | Cook time: 6 to 10 hours | Serves 4 to 6

- 6 medium potatoes, sliced
- 1 large onion, thinly sliced
- 2 tablespoons olive oil
- 2 cups shredded Mozzarella cheese
- 2 ounces (57 g) sliced pepperoni
- 1 teaspoon salt
- 1 (8-ounce / 227-g) can pizza sauce

1. In a skillet, heat the oil over medium heat and sauté the sliced potatoes and onions until the onions become transparent. Drain the excess oil well. 2. Transfer the sautéed potatoes and onions to the Ninja Foodi PossibleCooker. Add the shredded cheese, pepperoni, and a pinch of salt, mixing to combine evenly. 3. Pour the pizza sauce over the top, spreading it to cover the ingredients. 4. Cover the Ninja Foodi PossibleCooker and cook on low for 6 to 10 hours, or until the potatoes are tender.

Buttery Sage and Parsley Fingerling Potatoes

Prep time: 15 minutes | Cook time: 4 to 5 hours | Serves 6

- 2½ pounds (1.1 kg) fingerling potatoes, scrubbed and cut in half
- ½ cup (1 stick) unsalted butter, melted
- ¼ cup olive oil
- 6 fresh sage leaves, finely chopped
- 1½ teaspoons salt
- ½ teaspoon freshly ground black pepper
- ¼ cup finely chopped fresh Italian parsley, for garnish
- ¼ cup freshly grated Parmesan cheese, for garnish

1. Put the potatoes in the insert of a 5- to 7-quart Ninja Foodi PossibleCooker. Add the butter, oil, sage, salt, and pepper and stir to distribute the ingredients. Cover and cook on low for 4 to 5 hours, until the potatoes are tender. 2. Combine the parsley and cheese in a small bowl and sprinkle over the top of the potatoes. 3. Serve the potatoes immediately.

Garlic and Rosemary Infused Red Potatoes

Prep time: 10 minutes | Cook time: 4 hours | Serves 8

- ½ cup extra-virgin olive oil
- 6 cloves garlic, sliced
- 2 teaspoons fresh rosemary leaves, finely chopped
- 2 teaspoons coarse salt
- 1 teaspoon coarsely ground black pepper
- 16 to 20 small (2-inch) red potatoes, scrubbed

1. Combine all the ingredients in the insert of a 5- to 7-quart Ninja Foodi PossibleCooker cover and cook on high for 4 hours, stirring after 2 hours to bring the potatoes from the bottom to the top. 2. Serve immediately, or keep warm for up to 2 hours in the cooker set on warm.

Classic Eggplant Parmigiana Casserole

Prep time: 30 minutes | Cook time: 4½ hours | Serves 6 to 8

- 1 large purple eggplant, peeled and cut into ½-inch rounds
- 3 tablespoons salt
- Garlic Marinara Sauce:
- 2 tablespoons extra-virgin olive oil
- 4 cloves garlic, minced
- Pinch of red pepper flakes
- 2 teaspoons dried basil
- 1 (28- to 32-ounce / 794- to 907-g) can crushed tomatoes
- ½ cup finely chopped fresh Italian parsley
- 1½ teaspoons salt
- ½ teaspoon freshly ground black pepper
- 1 teaspoon sugar
- 8 ounces (227 g) fresh Mozzarella, cut into ¼-inch-thick slices
- 1 cup freshly grated Asiago cheese
- 1 cup freshly grated Parmigiano-Reggiano cheese

1. Arrange the eggplant slices on a baking sheet lined with paper towels. Salt the eggplant generously. (This step will remove the excess water from the eggplant, giving you a nice dish rather than a Ninja Foodi PossibleCooker full of water). After 10 minutes, turn the eggplant and salt the other side. Let stand for another 10 minutes. Blot the slices dry with paper towels and set aside while making the sauce. 2. Heat the oil in a small saucepan over medium-high heat. Add the garlic, red pepper flakes, and basil and sauté until the garlic is fragrant but not browned, about 1 minute. Stir in the tomatoes, parsley, salt, pepper, and sugar; simmer uncovered for 30 minutes. Taste and adjust the seasoning. 3. Coat the insert of a 5- to 7-quart Ninja Foodi PossibleCooker with nonstick cooking spray or line it with a slow-cooker liner according to the manufacturer's directions. 4. Spread a layer of the sauce on the bottom of the slow-cooker insert, then top with a layer of the eggplant. Spread an even layer of the Mozzarella over the eggplant and sprinkle with some of the Asiago and Parmigiano. Top with a bit of the sauce. Continue to layer the sauce, eggplant, and cheeses, ending with the last bit of Asiago and Parmigiano. 5. Cover and cook on low for 4 hours, until the casserole is heated through and the cheese is melted in the center. Allow the casserole to rest for 10 minutes before serving.

Uptown Scalloped Potatoes

Prep time: 15 minutes | Cook time: 6 to 7 hours | Serves 8 to 10

- 5 pounds (2.3 kg) red potatoes, peeled and sliced
- 2 cups water
- 1 teaspoon cream of tartar
- ¼ pound (113 g) bacon, cut
- in 1-inch squares, browned until crisp, and drained
- Dash of salt
- ½ pint whipping cream
- 1 pint half-and-half

1. Toss the sliced potatoes in water mixed with cream of tartar to prevent browning, then drain well. 2. In a large Ninja Foodi PossibleCooker, layer the potatoes and chopped bacon, sprinkling lightly with salt between the layers. 3. In a separate bowl, mix the whipping cream and half-and-half until well combined, then pour over the potatoes and bacon in the Ninja Foodi PossibleCooker. 4. Cover and cook on low for 6 to 7 hours, or until the potatoes are tender and the flavors are well blended.

Fruity Sweet Potatoes

Prep time: 15 minutes | Cook time: 6 to 8 hours | Serves 6

- 2 pounds (907 g) sweet potatoes or yams
- 1½ cups applesauce
- ⅔ cup brown sugar
- 3 tablespoons butter, melted
- 1 teaspoon cinnamon
- Chopped nuts (optional)

1. Peel the sweet potatoes if desired, then cut them into cubes or slices and place them in the Ninja Foodi PossibleCooker. 2. In a separate bowl, mix the applesauce, brown sugar, melted butter, and cinnamon until well combined. Spoon this mixture over the sweet potatoes in the Ninja Foodi PossibleCooker. 3. Cover and cook on low for 6 to 8 hours, or until the sweet potatoes are tender. 4. If you prefer, mash the sweet potatoes together with the sauce using a large spoon, or transfer the sweet potatoes to a serving dish and drizzle the sauce on top. 5. Sprinkle with chopped nuts if desired, and serve warm.

Creamy Corn Bake

Prep time: 5 minutes | Cook time: 3 hours | Serves 8

- 1 quart corn (be sure to thaw and drain if using frozen corn)
- 2 eggs, beaten
- 1 teaspoon salt
- 1 cup fat-free milk
- ⅛ teaspoon black pepper
- 2 teaspoons oil
- 2 tablespoons sugar
- 3 tablespoons flour

1. Combine all ingredients well. Pour into Ninja Foodi PossibleCooker sprayed with fat-free cooking spray. 2. Cover. Cook on high 3 hours.

All-American Tomato Stew

Prep time: 15 minutes | Cook time: 8 hours | Serves 6 to 8

- 2 tablespoons olive oil
- 1 medium onion, coarsely chopped
- 1 medium green bell pepper, seeded and coarsely chopped
- 10 large tomatoes, peeled, cored, and cut into wedges
- 3 tablespoons brown sugar
- 1½ teaspoons salt
- ½ teaspoon freshly ground black pepper

1. Combine all the ingredients in the insert of a 5- to 7-quart Ninja Foodi PossibleCooker. Cover and cook on low for 8 hours, until the tomatoes are tender. 2. Allow the tomatoes to cool before serving.

Cranberry-Orange Beets

Prep time: 15 minutes | Cook time: 3½ to 7½ hours | Serves 6

- 2 pounds (907 g) medium beets, peeled and quartered
- ½ teaspoon ground nutmeg
- 1 cup cranberry juice
- 1 teaspoon orange peel,
- finely shredded (optional)
- 2 tablespoons butter
- 2 tablespoons sugar
- 4 teaspoons cornstarch

1. Place the beets in the Ninja Foodi PossibleCooker and sprinkle them with nutmeg. 2. Pour in the cranberry juice and add the orange peel. Dot the beets with butter for added flavor. 3. Cover and cook on low for 6 to 7 hours, or on high for 3 to 3½ hours, until the beets are tender. 4. In a small bowl, combine the sugar and cornstarch. 5. Remove ½ cup of the cooking liquid from the Ninja Foodi PossibleCooker and stir it into the cornstarch mixture until smooth. 6. Add the cornstarch mixture back into the Ninja Foodi

PossibleCooker, stirring to combine. 7. Cover and cook on high for an additional 15 to 30 minutes, or until the sauce thickens.

Potato Filling

Prep time: 40 minutes | Cook time: 3 hours | Serves 20

- 1 cup celery, chopped fine
- 1 medium onion, minced
- ½ cup butter
- 2 (15-ounce / 425-g) packages low-fat bread cubes
- 6 eggs, beaten
- 1 quart fat-free milk
- 1 quart mashed potatoes
- 3 teaspoons salt
- 2 pinches saffron
- 1 cup boiling water
- 1 teaspoon black pepper

1. In a skillet, melt the butter over medium heat and sauté the chopped celery and onion until they become transparent. 2. Transfer the sautéed vegetables to a large bowl and combine with the bread cubes. Mix in the remaining ingredients, adding more milk if the mixture appears dry to ensure it's sufficiently moist. 3. Pour the stuffing mixture into a large Ninja Foodi PossibleCooker or divide among several medium-sized Ninja Foodi PossibleCookers. Cook on high for 3 hours, stirring from the bottom every hour to prevent sticking.

Herbed Parsley Smashed Red Potatoes

Prep time: 20 minutes | Cook time: 6 hours | Serves 8

- 16 small red potatoes
- 1 celery rib, sliced
- 1 medium carrot, sliced
- ¼ cup finely chopped onion
- 2 cups chicken broth
- 1 tablespoon minced fresh parsley
- 1½ teaspoons salt, divided
- 1 teaspoon pepper, divided
- 1 garlic clove, minced
- 2 tablespoons butter, melted
- Additional minced fresh parsley

1. Place potatoes, celery, carrot and onion in a 4-quart Ninja Foodi PossibleCooker. In a small bowl, mix broth, parsley, 1 teaspoon salt, ½ teaspoon pepper and garlic; pour over vegetables. Cook, covered, on low 6 to 8 hours or until potatoes are tender. 2. Transfer potatoes from Ninja Foodi PossibleCooker to a 15x10x1-inch pan; discard cooking liquid and vegetables. Using the bottom of a measuring cup, flatten potatoes slightly. Transfer to a large bowl; drizzle with butter. Sprinkle with remaining salt and pepper; toss to coat. Sprinkle with additional parsley.

Tangy Hot German Potato Salad

Prep time: 20 minutes | Cook time: 3 to 8 hours | Serves 8

- 6 to 7 cups potatoes, sliced
- 1 cup onions, chopped
- 1 cup celery, chopped
- 1 cup water
- ⅓ cup vinegar
- ¼ cup sugar
- 2 tablespoons quick-cooking tapioca
- 1 teaspoon salt
- 1 teaspoon celery seed
- ¼ teaspoon black pepper
- 6 slices lean turkey bacon, cooked and crumbled
- ¼ cup fresh parsley

1. Combine potatoes, onions, and celery in Ninja Foodi PossibleCooker. 2. In a bowl, combine water, vinegar, sugar, tapioca, salt, celery seed, and black pepper. 3. Pour over potatoes. Mix together gently. 4. Cover. Cook on low 6 to 8 hours, or on high 3 to 4 hours. 5. Stir in bacon and parsley just before serving.

Caponata

Prep time: 25 minutes | Cook time: 6 hours | Serves 6

- 2 tablespoons extra-virgin olive oil
- 1 medium red onion, finely chopped
- 3 cloves garlic, minced
- 3 stalks celery, finely chopped
- 2 medium purple eggplants, finely diced
- 2 medium red bell peppers, seeded and cut into ½-inch pieces
- 1 teaspoon dried oregano
- 1 teaspoon salt
- Pinch of red pepper flakes
- ¼ cup balsamic vinegar
- 1 (15-ounce / 425-g) can diced tomatoes, with their juice
- 1 cup golden raisins
- ¼ cup brined capers, drained
- ½ cup pitted Kalamata olives (or your favorite olive)
- ½ cup finely chopped fresh Italian parsley

1. Heat the oil in a large skillet over medium-high heat. Add the chopped onion, minced garlic, and diced celery, sautéing for about 3 minutes until the onion becomes soft. 2. Transfer the sautéed mixture to the insert of a 5- to 7-quart Ninja Foodi PossibleCooker. In the same skillet, add the diced eggplants, bell peppers, oregano, salt, and red pepper flakes, cooking until the eggplant starts to soften, about 4 to 5 minutes. Pour in the vinegar, allowing it to evaporate slightly, then stir in the diced tomatoes and raisins. 3. Transfer everything from the skillet to the slow-cooker insert, stirring to combine all the ingredients well. Cover and cook on low for 5 hours. 4. Stir in the capers, chopped olives, and parsley, and continue to cook for an additional hour, or until the eggplant is tender. 5. Remove the caponata from the Ninja Foodi PossibleCooker and serve it cold or at room temperature, as desired.

Savory Onion-Seasoned Roasted Potatoes

Prep time: 20 minutes | Cook time: 5 to 6 hours | Serves 6

- 6 medium potatoes, diced
- ⅓ cup olive oil
- 1 envelope dry onion soup mix

1. Combine potatoes and olive oil in plastic bag. Shake well. 2. Add onion soup mix. Shake well. 3. Pour into Ninja Foodi PossibleCooker. 4. Cover and cook on low 5 to 6 hours.

Zucchini, Tomato, and Leek Gratin

Prep time: 20 minutes | Cook time: 2½ to 3 hours | Serves 6 to 8

- 4 cup shredded zucchini
- 3 teaspoons salt
- 3 medium tomatoes, cut into ½-inch-thick slices
- 2 leeks, coarsely chopped, using the white and tender green parts
- 4 tablespoons extra-virgin olive oil
- 2 teaspoons dried tarragon
- ½ teaspoon freshly ground black pepper
- 2 tablespoons tomato paste
- ½ cup chicken broth
- Freshly grated Parmigiano-Reggiano cheese, for garnish

1. Place the zucchini slices in a colander, sprinkle with 1 teaspoon of the salt, and press out as much moisture as possible. Sprinkle the tomato slices with 1 teaspoon of salt and let them drain on paper towels to remove excess liquid. 2. Toss the sliced leeks with 2 tablespoons of the olive oil. Drizzle the remaining 2 tablespoons of oil into the insert of a 5- to 7-quart Ninja Foodi PossibleCooker. In a small bowl, mix together the tarragon, black pepper, tomato paste, remaining salt, and broth. Arrange a layer of salted tomatoes in the Ninja Foodi PossibleCooker, then spoon 2 tablespoons of the tomato paste mixture over them. Add a layer of zucchini, sprinkle with another 2 tablespoons of the tomato paste mixture, and layer some of the leeks on top. Repeat this layering process, finishing by pouring the remaining tomato paste mixture over the vegetables. 3. Cover the Ninja Foodi PossibleCooker and cook on high for 1½ to 2 hours, or until the vegetables are tender. Uncover and cook on low for an additional hour to let the flavors develop further. 4. Serve the vegetable gratin warm or at room temperature, garnished with a sprinkling of grated Parmigiano-Reggiano.

Bavarian Cabbage

Prep time: 10 minutes | Cook time: 3 to 8 hours | Serves 4 to 8

- 1 small head red cabbage, sliced
- 1 medium onion, chopped
- 3 tart apples, cored and quartered
- 2 teaspoons salt
- 1 cup hot water
- 2 tablespoons sugar
- ⅓ cup vinegar
- 3 tablespoons bacon drippings

1. Layer all the ingredients in the Ninja Foodi PossibleCooker in the order they are listed. 2. Cover and cook on low for 8 hours or on high for 3 hours, until everything is fully cooked and flavors are blended. Stir well before serving to combine all the ingredients evenly.

Savory Turkish Stuffed Eggplant with Tomato and Herbs

Prep time: 15 minutes | Cook time: 2 to 4 hours | Serves 6

- ½ cup extra-virgin olive oil
- 3 small eggplants
- 1 teaspoon sea salt
- ½ teaspoon black pepper
- 1 large yellow onion, finely chopped
- 4 garlic cloves, minced
- 1 (15-ounce / 425-g) can
- diced tomatoes, with the juice
- ¼ cup finely chopped fresh flat-leaf parsley
- 6 (8-inch) round pita breads, quartered and toasted
- 1 cup plain Greek-style yogurt

1. Pour ¼ cup of the olive oil into the Ninja Foodi PossibleCooker, and generously coat the interior of the crock. 2. Cut each eggplant in half lengthwise. You can leave the stem on. Score the cut side of each half every ¼ inch, being careful not to cut through the skin. 3. Arrange the eggplant halves, skin-side down, in the Ninja Foodi PossibleCooker. Sprinkle with 1 teaspoon salt and ½ teaspoon pepper. 4. In a large skillet, heat the remaining ¼ cup olive oil over medium-high heat. Sauté the onion and garlic for 3 minutes, or until the onion begins to soften. 5. Add the tomatoes and parsley to the skillet. Season with salt and pepper. Sauté for another 5 minutes, until the liquid has almost evaporated. 6. Using a large spoon, spoon the tomato mixture over the eggplants, covering each half with some of the mixture. 7. Cover and cook on high for 2 hours or on low for 4 hours. When the dish is finished, the eggplant should feel very tender when you insert the tip of a sharp knife into the thickest part. 8. Uncover the Ninja Foodi PossibleCooker, and let the eggplant rest for 10 minutes. Then transfer the eggplant to a serving dish. If there is any juice in the bottom of the cooker, spoon it over the eggplant. Serve hot with toasted pita wedges and yogurt on the side.

South-of-the-Border Stewed Tomatoes

Prep time: 15 minutes | Cook time: 8 hours | Serves 6

- 2 tablespoons olive oil
- 1 medium onion, coarsely chopped
- 2 Anaheim chiles, seeded and coarsely chopped
- 1 teaspoon ground cumin
- 1 teaspoon dried oregano
- 2 tablespoons sugar
- 1½ teaspoons salt
- 10 large tomatoes, peeled, cored, and cut into wedges

1. Heat the oil in a large skillet over medium-high heat. Add the chopped onion, chiles, cumin, and oregano, sautéing for 4 to 5 minutes until the onion starts to soften. 2. Transfer the sautéed mixture to the insert of a 5- to 7-quart Ninja Foodi PossibleCooker. Stir in the sugar, salt, and tomatoes, making sure everything is well combined. Cover and cook on low for 8 hours, allowing the flavors to meld. 3. Let the tomato mixture cool slightly before serving.

Crispy Pancetta and Shaved Brussels Sprouts

Prep time: 10 minutes | Cook time: 1½ hours | Serves 6

- ½ cup extra-virgin olive oil
- 3 ounces (85 g) pancetta, finely chopped
- 3 cloves garlic, sliced
- 2 pounds (907 g) Brussels
- sprouts, ends trimmed, cut into quarters, and leaves separated
- 1½ teaspoons salt
- ½ teaspoon freshly ground black pepper

1. Heat the oil in a medium sauté pan over high heat. Add the pancetta and cook until crispy. Remove it to paper towels to drain. Add the garlic to the pan and cook over low heat until it begins to turn golden, being careful not to let it get brown. 2. Pour the oil and garlic into the insert of a 5- to 7-quart Ninja Foodi PossibleCooker. Stir in the sprouts, salt, and pepper. cover and cook on high for 1 hour, until the leaves are tender. Stir in the pancetta and cook for another 30 minutes. 3. Serve hot or at room temperature.

Ranch Potatoes

- 6 bacon strips, chopped
- 2½ pounds (1.1 kg) small red potatoes, cubed
- 1 (8-ounce / 227-g) package cream cheese, softened
- 1 (10¾-ounce / 305-g) can condensed cream of potato
- soup, undiluted
- ¼ cup 2% milk
- 1 envelope buttermilk ranch salad dressing mix
- 3 tablespoons thinly sliced green onions

1. In a large skillet over medium heat, cook the bacon until crispy, stirring occasionally. Use a slotted spoon to transfer the bacon to paper towels to drain. Reserve 1 tablespoon of the bacon drippings and discard the rest. 2. Place the potatoes into a 3-quart Ninja Foodi PossibleCooker. In a separate bowl, beat together the cream cheese, condensed soup, milk, dressing mix, and reserved bacon drippings until well blended. Stir this mixture into the potatoes in the Ninja Foodi PossibleCooker, then sprinkle the cooked bacon over the top. 3. Cover and cook on low for 7 to 8 hours, or until the potatoes are tender. Just before serving, top with chopped green onions.

Eggplant and Zucchini Casserole

- 2 egg whites
- 1 medium eggplant
- 1 medium zucchini
- 1½ cups bread crumbs
- 1 teaspoon garlic powder
- 1 teaspoon low-sodium
- Italian seasoning
- 1 (48-ounce / 1.4-kg) jar fat-free, low-sodium spaghetti sauce
- 1 (8-ounce / 227-g) bag low-fat shredded Mozzarella cheese

1. In a small bowl, beat the egg whites until frothy. 2. Slice the eggplant and zucchini and place the slices into a separate bowl. 3. In another bowl, mix together the bread crumbs, garlic powder, and Italian seasoning. 4. Dip each slice of eggplant and zucchini into the egg whites, then coat them in the bread crumb mixture. Layer the coated vegetables in the Ninja Foodi PossibleCooker, pouring marinara sauce and sprinkling shredded cheese over each layer. Reserve ½ cup of cheese for later. Pour any remaining sauce over

the top layer. 5. Cover and cook on low for 5 to 6 hours, or until the vegetables are tender. 6. During the last 15 minutes of cooking, sprinkle the reserved ½ cup of cheese over the top and let it melt. Serve warm.

Sweet and Savory Tzimmes with Dried Fruits

- 1 to 2 sweet potatoes
- 6 carrots, sliced
- 1 potato, peeled and diced
- 1 onion, chopped
- 2 apples, peeled and sliced
- 1 butternut squash, peeled and sliced
- ¼ cup dry white wine or apple juice
- ½ pound (227 g) dried apricots
- 1 tablespoon ground cinnamon
- 1 tablespoon apple pie spice
- 1 tablespoon maple syrup or honey
- 1 teaspoon salt
- 1 teaspoon ground ginger

1. Combine all ingredients in large Ninja Foodi PossibleCooker, or mix all ingredients in large bowl and then divide between 2 (4- to 5-quart) cookers. 2. Cover. Cook on low 10 hours.

Squash and Apples

- 1 large butternut squash, peeled, seeded, and cut into ¼-inch slices
- 2 medium cooking apples, cored and cut into ¼-inch slices
- 3 tablespoons raisins (optional)
- 3 tablespoons reduced-calorie pancake syrup
- ¼ cup apple cider or apple juice

1. In the Ninja Foodi PossibleCooker, layer half of the sliced squash, apple slices, and raisins. 2. Drizzle half of the syrup over the layered ingredients. 3. Repeat the layers with the remaining squash, apples, and raisins, then drizzle with the remaining syrup. 4. Pour the apple cider over the top. 5. Cover and cook on low for 6 to 8 hours, or until the squash is tender. Serve warm.

Chapter 9

9

Desserts

Chapter 9 Desserts

Spiced Caramel Apples

Prep time: 15 minutes | Cook time: 4 to 6 hours | Serves 4

- 4 very large tart apples, cored
- ½ cup apple juice
- 8 tablespoons brown sugar
- 12 hot cinnamon candies
- 4 tablespoons butter
- 8 caramel candies
- ¼ teaspoon ground cinnamon
- Whipped cream

1. Remove ½-inch-wide strip of peel off the top of each apple and place apples in Ninja Foodi PossibleCooker. 2. Pour apple juice over apples. 3. Fill the center of each apple with 2 tablespoons brown sugar, 3 hot cinnamon candies, 1 tablespoon butter, and 2 caramel candies. Sprinkle with cinnamon. 4. Cover and cook on low 4 to 6 hours, or until tender. 5. Serve hot with whipped cream.

Creamy Tropical Rice Pudding

Prep time: 10 minutes | Cook time: 5 hours | Serves 2

- Nonstick cooking spray
- 1 cup short-grain white rice
- 5 cups milk
- 1 cup light cream
- ½ cup sugar
- 1 tablespoon butter
- 2 teaspoons vanilla
- ½ cup chopped mango
- ½ cup chopped peeled kiwi

1. Spray the Ninja Foodi PossibleCooker with the nonstick cooking spray. 2. In the Ninja Foodi PossibleCooker, combine all the ingredients except the mango and kiwi, and stir. 3. Cover and cook on low for 5 hours, or until the rice is tender and the pudding is thick. If you are home, stir it a few times while it's cooking. 4. Top with the mango and kiwi and serve.

Tapioca

Prep time: 10 minutes | Cook time: 3½ hours | Serves 10 to 12

- 2 quarts whole milk
- 1¼ cups sugar
- 1 cup dry small pearl tapioca
- 4 eggs
- 1 teaspoon vanilla
- Whipped topping (optional)

1. In the Ninja Foodi PossibleCooker, combine the milk and sugar, stirring until the sugar is as dissolved as possible. Add the tapioca and stir well to mix. 2. Cover and cook on high for 3 hours, stirring occasionally to prevent sticking. 3. In a small mixing bowl, lightly beat the eggs, then add the vanilla extract and about 1 cup of the hot milk mixture from the Ninja Foodi PossibleCooker. Whisk until well combined, then stir the egg mixture back into the Ninja Foodi PossibleCooker. 4. Cover and cook on high for an additional 20 minutes, or until the pudding thickens. 5. Allow the tapioca pudding to chill in the refrigerator for several hours. Serve cold, topped with whipped cream if desired.

Crunchy Candy Clusters

Prep time: 15 minutes | Cook time: 1 hour | Makes 6½ dozen

- 2 pounds (907 g) white candy coating, coarsely chopped
- 1½ cups peanut butter
- ½ teaspoon almond extract
- (optional)
- 4 cups Cap'n Crunch cereal
- 4 cups crisp rice cereal
- 4 cups miniature marshmallows

1. Place the candy coating into a 5-quart Ninja Foodi PossibleCooker. Cover and cook on high for 1 hour, or until melted. Add the peanut butter and stir until smooth. If desired, stir in the extract for extra flavor. 2. In a large mixing bowl, combine the cereals and marshmallows. Pour the melted peanut butter mixture over the cereal mix and stir until everything is well coated. 3. Drop spoonfuls of the mixture onto waxed paper and let them stand until fully set. Store at room temperature in an airtight container.

Tropical Coconut Macadamia Bread Pudding

Prep time: 25 minutes | Cook time: 4½ hours | Serves 8 to 10

- 8 cups 1-inch cubes or torn stale sturdy white bread, such as Pepperidge Farm
- 1½ cups shredded sweetened coconut
- 1 cup chopped macadamia nuts
- 1½ cups milk-chocolate chips, such as Ghirardelli or Guittard
- 1 (13- to 14-ounce / 369- to 397-g) can coconut milk
- 1 cup milk
- 1 cup heavy cream
- 8 large eggs
- ½ cup firmly packed light brown sugar
- ¼ cup dark rum (optional)
- Hot fudge, berry, or buttered rum sauce for serving

1. Coat the insert of a 5- to 7-quart Ninja Foodi PossibleCooker with nonstick cooking spray. Put the bread, coconut, macadamia nuts, and chocolate chips in a large bowl. In another bowl, whisk together the coconut milk, milk, cream, eggs, sugar, and rum (if using). 2. Pour the milk mixture over the bread and stir until the bread is soaked. Transfer the bread mixture to the slow-cooker insert. Cover and cook on low for 4 hours, until the pudding is cooked through and an instant-read thermometer inserted in the center reads 170ºF (77ºC). Uncover and cook for an additional 30 minutes. 3. Serve the pudding with hot fudge sauce, berry sauce, or buttered rum sauce.

Hot Fudge Upside-Down Cake

Prep time: 20 minutes | Cook time: 2 hours | Serves 4 to 6

- ½ cup milk
- 3 tablespoons unsalted butter, melted
- 1 teaspoon vanilla bean paste
- 1 cup granulated sugar
- 1 cup all-purpose flour
- ½ cup cocoa powder (make sure to use natural cocoa
- powder and not Dutch process)
- 2 teaspoons baking powder
- ¾ cup firmly packed light brown sugar
- 1¾ cups boiling water
- Vanilla ice cream or unsweetened whipped cream for serving

1. Coat the insert of a 5- to 7-quart Ninja Foodi PossibleCooker with nonstick cooking spray. In a mixing bowl, stir together the milk, melted butter, and vanilla bean paste. Gradually add the granulated sugar, flour, ¼ cup of the cocoa powder, and baking powder, mixing until smooth. Spread the batter evenly in the prepared slow-cooker insert. 2. In a small bowl, combine the brown sugar and the remaining ¼ cup of cocoa powder, sprinkling the mixture evenly over the batter. Carefully pour the boiling water over the top without stirring. Cover and cook on high for 2 hours, or until a skewer inserted into the center comes out clean. Uncover and let the dessert cool for about 20 minutes. 3. Serve warm in bowls with a scoop of vanilla ice cream.

Apple Cranberry Crumble

Prep time: 20 minutes | Cook time: 2 to 2½ hours | Serves 10

- 5 large apples, peeled and sliced
- 1 cup fresh or frozen cranberries, thawed
- ¾ cup packed brown sugar, divided
- 2 tablespoons lemon juice
- ½ cup all-purpose flour
- Dash salt
- ⅓ cup cold butter
- Vanilla ice cream
- Toasted chopped pecans

1. In a greased 5-quart Ninja Foodi PossibleCooker, combine apples, cranberries, ¼ cup brown sugar and lemon juice. In a small bowl, mix flour, salt and remaining brown sugar; cut in butter until crumbly. Sprinkle over fruit mixture. 2. Cook, covered, on high 2 to 2½ hours or until apples are tender. Serve with ice cream and pecans.

Warm Spiced Stuffed Apples with Figs and Walnuts

Prep time: 10 minutes | Cook time: 2 to 5 hours | Serves 4

- 4 medium-sized tart cooking apples (like Granny Smith or Braeburn)
- ⅓ cup finely chopped dried figs or raisins
- ½ cup finely chopped walnuts
- ¼ cup packed light brown sugar
- ½ teaspoon apple pie spice or cinnamon
- ¼ cup apple juice
- 1 tablespoon butter, cut into 4 pieces

1. Core the apples. Cut a strip of peel from the top of each apple. Place the apples upright in the Ninja Foodi PossibleCooker. 2. In a small bowl, combine figs, walnuts, brown sugar, and apple pie spice. Spoon the mixture into the center of the apples, patting in with a knife or a narrow metal spatula. 3. Pour the apple juice around the apples in the Ninja Foodi PossibleCooker. 4. Top each apple with a piece of butter. 5. Cover and cook on low for 4 to 5 hours or on high for 2 to 2½ hours until very tender. 6. Serve warm, with some of the cooking liquid spooned over the apples.

Spiced Fruit Compote

Prep time: 30 minutes | Cook time: 3 to 8 hours | Serves 10 to 12

- 3 medium-size pears, peeled, cored, and cubed
- 1 (16-ounce / 454-g) can pineapple, in cubes or chunks, with the juice
- 1 cup quartered dried apricots
- 3 tablespoons frozen orange juice concentrate
- 2 tablespoons packed light brown sugar
- 1 tablespoon quick-cooking tapioca
- 1 teaspoon grated peeled fresh ginger (or ½ teaspoon dried ground ginger)
- 2 cups pitted dark, sweet cherries
- 1 cup toasted shredded unsweetened coconut
- 1 cup chopped and toasted macadamia nuts or pecans

1. In the Ninja Foodi PossibleCooker, combine the sliced pears, pineapple and its juice, chopped apricots, orange juice concentrate, brown sugar, tapioca, and ginger, stirring well to mix all the ingredients. 2. Cover the Ninja Foodi PossibleCooker and cook on low for 6 to 8 hours or on high for 3 to 4 hours. About 30 minutes before the cooking time is finished, gently stir in the cherries. 3. Serve the warm fruit mixture topped with shredded coconut and chopped nuts. Enjoy!

Blood Orange Upside-Down Spice Cake

Prep time: 25 minutes | Cook time: 4 hours | Serves 6 to 8

Orange Layer:

- 5 tablespoons unsalted butter, cut into small pieces, plus more for Ninja Foodi PossibleCooker crock
- ¾ cup firmly packed dark brown sugar
- 3 tablespoons dark rum

Cake:

- ¾ cups cake flour
- ¾ teaspoons baking powder
- ½ teaspoon ground cinnamon
- ¼ teaspoon ground nutmeg
- ¼ teaspoon salt
- 4 tablespoons unsalted butter, at room temperature
- 2 pounds (907 g) blood oranges (about 6), sliced, peeled, with all of the bitter white pith removed
- ½ teaspoon ground cardamom

- ⅔ cup granulated sugar
- 1 egg, at room temperature
- 1 egg yolk, at room temperature
- 2 tablespoons whole milk, at room temperature
- 2 cups vanilla ice cream, for serving (optional)

Make the Orange Layer: 1. Butter the inside of the Ninja Foodi PossibleCooker crock, line completely with foil, and then butter the foil. 2. Sprinkle the butter, brown sugar, and rum over the foil on the bottom of the Ninja Foodi PossibleCooker. Cover that with the orange slices in a slightly overlapping pattern, and sprinkle with the cardamom. Press the oranges into the sugar. Make the Cake: 3. Sift the flour, baking powder, cinnamon, nutmeg, and salt into a large bowl. Whisk gently to combine evenly. 4. In a medium bowl, slowly beat the butter and sugar with an electric mixer until just blended. Raise the speed to high and beat until light and fluffy, scraping down the sides of the bowl occasionally, about 10 minutes. 5. Beat the egg and then the egg yolk into the butter-sugar mixture, allowing each to be fully incorporated before adding the next. 6. While mixing slowly, add the flour mixture to the butter-sugar mixture in three parts, alternating with the milk in two parts, beginning and ending with the flour. Mix briefly at medium speed to make a smooth batter. 7. Pour the batter over the oranges in the Ninja Foodi PossibleCooker and smooth with a spatula to even it out. 8. Lay a doubled length of paper towel from end to end over the top of the Ninja Foodi PossibleCooker, to line the lid and create a tighter seal. 9. Cover the cake tightly with the lid and cook on high until the cake begins to brown slightly on the sides and springs back when touched in the middle, about 3½ hours. Turn off the Ninja Foodi PossibleCooker and let the cake set, uncovered, about 20 minutes more. 10. Using the foil, lift the cake from the Ninja Foodi PossibleCooker and set on the counter to cool, about 30 minutes more. Fold back the foil, and carefully invert the cake onto a platter so the caramelized oranges are visible on top. 11. Slice or spoon the cake into bowls, and serve with ice cream, if desired.

Rich Double Chocolate Ninja Foodi PossibleCooker Bread Pudding

Prep time: 25 minutes | Cook time: 3 hours | Serves 2

- Nonstick cooking spray
- 6 cups cubed French bread
- 1 cup semisweet chocolate chips
- 2 cups chocolate milk
- 4 eggs, beaten
- 3 tablespoons butter, melted
- ½ cup brown sugar
- ¼ cup granulated sugar
- 3 tablespoons cocoa powder
- 2 teaspoons vanilla

1. Line the Ninja Foodi PossibleCooker with heavy-duty foil, and spray with the nonstick cooking spray. 2. In the Ninja Foodi PossibleCooker, combine the French bread and chocolate chips. 3. In a large bowl, beat all the remaining ingredients. Pour the mixture into the Ninja Foodi PossibleCooker. 4. Push the bread under the liquid. Let stand for 20 minutes. 5. Cover and cook on low for 3 hours, or until the mixture is set and reads 160°F (71°C) on a food thermometer, and serve.

"Baked" Custard

- 2 cups whole milk
- 3 eggs, slightly beaten
- ⅓ cup plus ½ teaspoon

- sugar, divided
- 1 teaspoon vanilla
- ¼ teaspoon cinnamon

1. In a small saucepan, heat the milk uncovered over medium heat until a skin forms on the surface. Remove from heat and allow the milk to cool slightly. 2. While the milk is cooling, combine the eggs, ⅓ cup sugar, and vanilla in a large mixing bowl, whisking until well blended. 3. Gradually stir the slightly cooled milk into the egg-sugar mixture, mixing thoroughly. 4. Pour the custard mixture into a greased 1-quart baking dish that fits into your Ninja Foodi PossibleCooker, or use a baking insert designed for slow-cooking. 5. In a small bowl, mix together the cinnamon and the reserved ½ teaspoon of sugar. Sprinkle this mixture evenly over the custard. 6. Cover the baking dish or insert tightly with foil. Place the container on a metal rack or trivet inside the Ninja Foodi PossibleCooker. Carefully pour hot water around the baking dish to reach a depth of about 1 inch. 7. Cover the Ninja Foodi PossibleCooker and cook on high for 2 to 3 hours, or until the custard is set. The custard is ready when a knife inserted into the center comes out clean. 8. Serve the custard warm directly from the baking dish or insert. Enjoy!

Piña Colada Bread Pudding

- 8 cups torn stale Hawaiian sweet egg bread, challah, or croissants
- 2 cups ½-inch chunks fresh pineapple
- 1 cup chopped macadamia nuts
- 1½ cups shredded

- sweetened coconut
- 3 cups heavy cream
- 8 large eggs
- 1 tablespoon vanilla extract or bean paste
- ¼ cup dark rum
- 1½ cups sugar

1. Coat the insert of a 5- to 7-quart Ninja Foodi PossibleCooker with nonstick cooking spray or line it with a slow-cooker liner as directed by the manufacturer. 2. Place the bread cubes into the slow-cooker insert and add the pineapple, chopped nuts, and shredded coconut, tossing to combine everything evenly. In a large mixing bowl, whisk together the cream, eggs, vanilla extract, rum, and sugar until well blended. Pour this mixture over the bread, pressing the bread down gently to make sure it is fully soaked. 3. Cover and cook on high for about 3 hours, or until the pudding is puffed and an instant-read thermometer inserted into the center

reads 185°F (85°C). Uncover and let the pudding cool for about 30 minutes. 4. Keep the Ninja Foodi PossibleCooker set on warm and serve directly from the cooker. Enjoy warm.

Cinnamon Stewed Apricots with Whipped Cream

- 1⅓ pounds (605 g) dried apricots, pitted
- 1 teaspoon ground cinnamon
- 1 cup granulated sugar

- 1 to 1¼ cups water
- ⅓ cup heavy cream
- 2 tablespoons toasted almond slivers

1. Turn the Ninja Foodi PossibleCooker to high and add the apricots, cinnamon, sugar, and water. 2. Cover and cook on high for 2 hours, or on low for 4 hours. 3. Leave to cool in a large bowl, then chill in the refrigerator. 4. Just before you're ready to serve, whip the cream. Serve chilled in individual glasses, topped with whipped cream and nuts.

Apple Cobbler

- Nonstick cooking spray
- 3 apples, peeled and sliced
- 1 tablespoon freshly squeezed lemon juice
- ½ cup dried cranberries
- ½ cup chopped walnuts
- ¼ cup granulated sugar, plus

- cup, divided
- ⅔ cup all-purpose flour
- ½ teaspoon baking powder
- 1 egg, beaten
- ⅔ cup milk
- 1 teaspoon vanilla

1. Spray the inside of the Ninja Foodi PossibleCooker with nonstick cooking spray to prevent sticking. 2. Add the sliced apples to the Ninja Foodi PossibleCooker, sprinkle them with lemon juice, and toss to coat. Add the cranberries and chopped walnuts, sprinkle with ¼ cup of granulated sugar, and toss again to distribute evenly. 3. In a medium bowl, mix together the flour, the remaining ⅓ cup of granulated sugar, baking powder, egg, milk, and vanilla extract until the batter is smooth. Spoon the batter over the apple mixture in the Ninja Foodi PossibleCooker, spreading it out evenly. 4. Cover and cook on low for 4 hours, or until the topping is fully set and cooked through. 5. Serve the warm dessert with cream or a scoop of ice cream. Enjoy!

Spiced Steamed Cucumber and Semolina Cake

Prep time: 15 minutes | Cook time: 2 to 3 hours | Serves 6 to 8

- 2 cups semolina flour
- 1½ pounds (680 g) cucumbers
- ½ teaspoon coconut oil
- 1 teaspoon baking powder, plus more for dusting
- 1½ cups grated jaggery (or dark-brown sugar)
- 2 cups freshly grated coconut
- 6 green cardamom pods, seeds only, pounded
- 3 tablespoons cashews, roughly crushed
- Pinch salt
- ½ teaspoon baking soda

1. Preheat the Ninja Foodi PossibleCooker on high. 2. In a large, dry frying pan, roast the semolina flour over low heat for 3 to 4 minutes, until it becomes aromatic. Remove from the pan and set aside. 3. Peel and grate the cucumbers into a large bowl. 4. Grease a pan (one that will fit inside your Ninja Foodi PossibleCooker) with the coconut oil and dust it with a pinch of baking powder. Set aside. 5. In a large bowl, mix the cucumber (with all its water), roasted semolina, jaggery, coconut, cardamom seeds, cashews, and salt into a batter. Add the baking powder and baking soda, and mix well. 6. Pour into the prepared cake pan. Cover the outside of the pan with foil. 7. Set a rack inside the Ninja Foodi PossibleCooker, or put some scrunched-up foil on the bottom. Pour in about 1 to 1¼ cups hot water and place the pan inside the cooker. Cover and cook on high for 2 to 3 hours. 8. Check if the cake is cooked by putting the tip of a knife into it. If it comes out clean, it's ready. 9. Leave to cool before removing the cake from the pan.

Apple-Pear Streusel

Prep time: 20 minutes | Cook time: 7 hours | Serves 2

- Nonstick cooking spray
- 4 apples, peeled and sliced
- 2 pears, peeled and sliced
- ¼ cup brown sugar
- 1 tablespoon freshly squeezed lemon juice
- ½ teaspoon ground cinnamon
- 2 tablespoons butter, plus 3 tablespoons cut into cubes, divided
- ½ cup light cream
- 1 cup all-purpose flour
- ½ cup rolled oats
- ½ cup chopped pecans
- ⅓ cup granulated sugar

1. Spray the inside of the Ninja Foodi PossibleCooker with nonstick cooking spray to prevent sticking. 2. In the Ninja Foodi PossibleCooker, combine the apple and pear slices. Sprinkle them with brown sugar, lemon juice, and cinnamon, then gently mix to combine. Dot the fruit with 2 tablespoons of butter and pour the cream evenly over the top. 3. In a medium bowl, mix together the flour, oats, chopped pecans, and granulated sugar. Add the remaining 3 tablespoons of butter in small cubes, and cut it into the mixture using two knives or a pastry blender until it resembles coarse crumbs. Sprinkle this crumb mixture evenly over the fruit layer in the Ninja Foodi PossibleCooker. 4. Cover and cook on low for 7 hours, or until the fruit is tender and the topping is golden. Enjoy warm!

Maple Creme Brulee

Prep time: 20 minutes | Cook time: 2 hours | Serves 3

- 1⅓ cups heavy whipping cream
- 3 egg yolks
- ½ cup packed brown sugar

Topping:

- 1½ teaspoons sugar
- ¼ teaspoon ground cinnamon
- ½ teaspoon maple flavoring
- 1½ teaspoons brown sugar

1. In a small saucepan, heat the cream over medium heat until bubbles begin to form around the edges. In a separate small bowl, whisk together the egg yolks, brown sugar, and cinnamon until well combined. Once the cream is heated, remove it from the heat and stir a small amount of the hot cream into the egg mixture to temper it. Gradually return the egg mixture to the saucepan, stirring constantly. Finally, stir in the maple flavoring. 2. Pour the custard mixture into three 6-ounce ramekins or custard cups. Place the ramekins in a 6-quart Ninja Foodi PossibleCooker and add boiling water around them, filling it to a depth of about 1 inch. Cover and cook on high for 2 to 2½ hours, or until the centers are just set (the mixture will jiggle slightly). Carefully remove the ramekins from the Ninja Foodi PossibleCooker and let them cool for 10 minutes. Cover and refrigerate for at least 4 hours to chill. 3. For the topping, mix the granulated sugar and brown sugar together. If you are using a crème brûlée torch, sprinkle the sugar mixture evenly over the top of each custard. Use the torch to heat the sugar until it caramelizes and forms a crispy top. Serve immediately. 4. If you prefer to broil the custards instead, place the ramekins on a baking sheet and let them stand at room temperature for 15 minutes. Sprinkle the sugar mixture over the tops, then broil about 8 inches from the heat for 3 to 5 minutes, or until the sugar is caramelized. Refrigerate for 1 to 2 hours until firm before serving. Enjoy!

Decadent Peach Melba Bread Pudding

Prep time: 20 minutes | Cook time: 3 hours | Serves 6 to 8

- 2 (16-ounce / 454-g) bags frozen unsweetened raspberries, defrosted and drained
- 1 cup superfine sugar
- 2 teaspoons fresh lemon juice
- 8 cups torn stale egg bread, challah, or croissants
- 12 medium peaches, peeled, pitted, and coarsely chopped, or 3 (16-ounce / 454-g) packages frozen peaches, defrosted, drained, and coarsely chopped
- 3 cups heavy cream
- 8 large eggs
- Grated zest of 1 orange
- ¼ cup Grand Marnier or other orange-flavored liqueur or 1 teaspoon orange extract
- 1½ cups granulated sugar

1. Coat the insert of a 5- to 7-quart Ninja Foodi PossibleCooker with nonstick cooking spray or line it with a slow-cooker liner according to the manufacturer's directions. 2. Heat the berries, superfine sugar, and lemon juice in a small saucepan until the mixture comes to a boil. Taste the syrup and add more sugar is it is too tart. Strain the mixture through a fine-mesh; you should have ⅔ to ¾ cup of syrup. Put the bread in the slow-cooker insert and stir in the peaches. Pour the raspberry syrup over all. 3. Whisk together the cream, eggs, orange zest, Grand Marnier, and granulated sugar in a large mixing bowl until blended. Pour over the bread in the slow-cooker insert and push the bread down to submerge it. 4. Cover and cook on high for about 3 hours, until puffed and an instant-read meat thermometer inserted in the center registers 185°F (85°C). Uncover and allow to cool for 30 minutes. 5. Serve from the cooker set on warm.

Blueberry Crisp

Prep time: 10 minutes | Cook time: 3 to 4 hours | Serves 8

- 5 tablespoons coconut oil, melted, divided
- 4 cups blueberries
- ¾ cup plus 2 tablespoons granulated erythritol
- 1 cup ground pecans
- 1 teaspoon baking soda
- ½ teaspoon ground cinnamon
- 2 tablespoons coconut milk
- 1 egg

1. Lightly grease the inside of a 4-quart Ninja Foodi PossibleCooker with 1 tablespoon of coconut oil. 2. Add the blueberries to the Ninja Foodi PossibleCooker insert and sprinkle with 2 tablespoons of erythritol, spreading them evenly. 3. In a large mixing bowl, combine the remaining ¾ cup erythritol, ground pecans, baking soda, and cinnamon, stirring until well mixed. 4. Add the coconut milk, egg, and the remaining coconut oil to the pecan mixture and stir until it forms coarse crumbs. 5. Spread the pecan mixture evenly over the blueberries in the Ninja Foodi PossibleCooker. 6. Cover and cook on low for 3 to 4 hours, or until the topping is golden and the blueberries are bubbly. 7. Serve the blueberry-pecan crumble warm. Enjoy!

Chapter 10

Pizzas, Wraps, and Sandwiches

Chapter 10 Pizzas, Wraps, and Sandwiches

Sweet and Tangy Polynesian Ham Sliders

Prep time: 20 minutes | Cook time: 3 hours | Serves 12

- 2 pounds (907 g) fully cooked ham, finely chopped
- 1 (20-ounce / 567-g) can crushed pineapple, undrained
- ¾ cup packed brown sugar
- ⅓ cup chopped green
- pepper
- ¼ cup Dijon mustard
- 1 green onion, chopped
- 1 tablespoon dried minced onion
- 12 hamburger buns or kaiser rolls, split

1. In a 3-quart Ninja Foodi PossibleCooker, combine the first seven ingredients. Cover and cook on low for 3 to 4 hours or until heated through. Using a slotted spoon, place ½ cup on each bun.

Barbecued Beef Sandwiches

Prep time: 10 minutes | Cook time: 10 to 12 hours | Makes 18 to 20 sandwiches

- 1 (3½- to 4-pound / 1.6- to 1.8-kg) beef round steak, cubed
- 1 cup finely chopped onions
- ½ cup firmly packed brown sugar
- 1 tablespoon chili powder
- ½ cup ketchup
- ⅓ cup cider vinegar
- 1 (12-ounce / 340-g) can beer
- 1 (6-ounce / 170-g) can tomato paste
- Buns

1. In the Ninja Foodi PossibleCooker, combine all ingredients except for the buns, stirring well to mix. 2. Cover the Ninja Foodi PossibleCooker and cook on low for 10 to 12 hours, allowing the flavors to meld and the beef to become tender. 3. Once cooked, use a slotted spoon to remove the beef from the sauce and transfer it to a large bowl. 4. Shred the beef using two forks, then add 2 cups of the sauce from the Ninja Foodi PossibleCooker to the shredded beef, mixing well to combine. 5. Pile the shredded beef onto the buns and serve immediately. Enjoy!

Garden-Fresh Beef and Veggie Sloppy Joes

Prep time: 35 minutes | Cook time: 5 hours | Serves 12

- 4 medium carrots, shredded (about 3½ cups)
- 1 medium yellow summer squash, shredded (about 2 cups)
- 1 medium zucchini, shredded (about 2 cups)
- 1 medium sweet red pepper, finely chopped
- 2 medium tomatoes, seeded and chopped
- 1 small red onion, finely chopped
- ½ cup ketchup
- 3 tablespoons minced fresh basil or 3 teaspoons dried basil
- 3 tablespoons molasses
- 2 tablespoons cider vinegar
- 2 garlic cloves, minced
- ½ teaspoon salt
- ½ teaspoon pepper
- 2 pounds (907 g) lean ground beef (90% lean)
- 12 whole wheat hamburger buns, split

1. In a 5- or 6-quart Ninja Foodi PossibleCooker, combine the first 13 ingredients. In a large skillet, cook beef over medium heat 8 to 10 minutes or until no longer pink, breaking into crumbles. Drain; transfer beef to Ninja Foodi PossibleCooker. Stir to combine. 2. Cook, covered, on low 5 to 6 hours or until heated through and vegetables are tender. Using a slotted spoon, serve beef mixture on buns.

Beach Boy's Pot Roast

Prep time: 10 minutes | Cook time: 8 to 12 hours | Makes 6 to 8 sandwiches

- 1 (3- to 4-pound / 1.4- to 1.8-kg) chuck or top round roast
- 8 to 12 slivers of garlic
- 1 (32-ounce / 907-g) jar
- pepperoncini peppers, undrained
- 6 to 8 large hoagie rolls
- 12 to 16 slices of your favorite cheese

1. Using a sharp knife, cut slits into the roast and insert garlic slivers into the slits for added flavor. 2. Place the seasoned beef in the Ninja Foodi PossibleCooker and spoon the peppers along with all of their juice over the top of the roast. 3. Cover the Ninja Foodi PossibleCooker and cook on low for 8 to 12 hours, or until the meat is tender but not dry. 4. Once cooked, carefully remove the meat from the Ninja Foodi PossibleCooker and allow it to cool slightly. Use two forks to shred the beef into bite-sized pieces. 5. Serve the shredded beef on hoagie rolls and top with your choice of cheese. Enjoy!

Middle-Eastern Sandwiches (for a crowd)

Prep time: 50 minutes | Cook time: 6 to 8 hours | Makes 10 to 16 sandwiches

- 4 pounds (1.8 kg) boneless beef or venison, cut in ½-inch cubes
- 4 tablespoons cooking oil
- 2 cups chopped onions
- 2 garlic cloves, minced
- 1 cup dry red wine
- 1 (6-ounce / 170-g) can tomato paste
- 1 teaspoon dried oregano
- 1 teaspoon dried basil
- ½ teaspoon dried rosemary
- 2 teaspoons salt
- Dash of pepper
- ¼ cup cold water
- ¼ cup cornstarch
- Pita pocket breads
- 2 cups shredded lettuce
- 1 large tomato, seeded and diced
- 1 large cucumber, seeded and diced
- 8 ounces (227 g) plain yogurt

1. In a skillet, brown the meat in 1 tablespoon of oil, cooking 1 pound (454 g) at a time. Reserve the drippings and transfer the browned meat to the Ninja Foodi PossibleCooker. 2. In the same skillet, sauté the onion and garlic in the reserved drippings until they are tender. Add this mixture to the meat in the Ninja Foodi PossibleCooker. 3. Pour in the wine, and stir in the tomato paste, oregano, basil, rosemary, salt, and pepper, mixing everything together well. 4. Cover the Ninja Foodi PossibleCooker and cook on low for 6 to 8 hours, allowing the flavors to develop. 5. When ready, turn the cooker to high. In a small bowl, combine the cornstarch and water, stirring until smooth. Gradually stir this mixture into the meat mixture in the Ninja Foodi PossibleCooker and cook until bubbly and thickened, stirring occasionally. 6. Split the pita breads to create pockets. Fill each pocket with the meat mixture, followed by lettuce, tomato, cucumber, and a dollop of yogurt. 7. Serve immediately and enjoy!

Italian-Style Turkey Sloppy Joes

Prep time: 15 minutes | Cook time: 3 to 4 hours | Makes 12 sandwiches

- 1½ pounds (680 g) ground turkey, browned in nonstick skillet
- 1 cup chopped onions
- 2 cups low-sodium tomato sauce
- 1 cup fresh mushrooms, sliced
- 2 tablespoons Splenda
- 1 to 2 tablespoons Italian seasoning, according to your taste preference
- 12 reduced-calorie hamburger buns
- 12 slices low-fat Mozzarella cheese (optional)

1. Place ground turkey, onions, tomato sauce, and mushrooms in Ninja Foodi PossibleCooker. 2. Stir in Splenda and Italian seasoning. 3. Cover. Cook on low 3 to 4 hours. 4. Serve ¼ cup of Sloppy Joe mixture on each bun, topped with cheese, if desired.

Classic Tangy Beef Sloppy Joes

Prep time: 15 minutes | Cook time: 3 to 10 hours | Makes 12 sandwiches

- 3 pounds (1.4 kg) ground beef, browned and drained
- 1 onion, finely chopped
- 1 green pepper, chopped
- 2 (8-ounce / 227-g) cans tomato sauce
- ¾ cup ketchup
- 1 tablespoon Worcestershire sauce
- 1 teaspoon chili powder
- ¼ teaspoon pepper
- ¼ teaspoon garlic powder
- Rolls, for serving

1. Combine all ingredients except rolls in Ninja Foodi PossibleCooker. 2. Cover. Cook on low 8 to 10 hours, or on high 3 to 4 hours. 3. Serve.

Savory Herbed French Dip Sandwiches

Prep time: 5 minutes | Cook time: 5 to 6 hours | Makes 6 to 8 sandwiches

- 1 (3-pound / 1.4-kg) chuck roast
- 2 cups water
- ½ cup soy sauce
- 1 teaspoon garlic powder
- 1 bay leaf
- 3 to 4 whole peppercorns
- 1 teaspoon dried rosemary (optional)
- 1 teaspoon dried thyme (optional)
- 6 to 8 French rolls

1. Place roast in Ninja Foodi PossibleCooker. 2. Combine remaining ingredients in a mixing bowl. Pour over meat. 3. Cover and cook on high 5 to 6 hours, or until meat is tender but not dry. 4. Remove meat from broth and shred with fork. Stir back into sauce. 5. Remove meat from the cooker by large forkfuls and place on French rolls.

Enchilada Pie

Prep time: 40 minutes | Cook time: 4 hours | Serves 8

- 1 (12-ounce / 340-g) package frozen vegetarian meat crumbles
- 1 cup chopped onion
- ½ cup chopped green pepper
- 2 teaspoons canola oil
- 1 (16-ounce / 454-g) can kidney beans, rinsed and drained
- 1 (15-ounce / 425-g) can black beans, rinsed and
- drained
- 1 (10-ounce / 283-g) can diced tomatoes and green chilies, undrained
- ½ cup water
- 1½ teaspoons chili powder
- ½ teaspoon ground cumin
- ¼ teaspoon pepper
- 6 whole wheat tortillas
- 2 cups shredded reduced-fat cheddar cheese

1. Cut three strips of heavy-duty foil measuring 25x3 inches and arrange them in a crisscross pattern at the bottom of a 5-quart Ninja Foodi PossibleCooker, resembling spokes on a wheel. Position the strips up the sides of the cooker and coat them with cooking spray to prevent sticking. 2. In a large saucepan, heat oil over medium heat and cook the meat crumbles, chopped onion, and green pepper until the vegetables are tender. Stir in both cans of beans, diced tomatoes, water, chili powder, cumin, and black pepper. Bring the mixture to a boil, then reduce the heat and let it simmer uncovered for 10 minutes. 3. In the prepared Ninja Foodi PossibleCooker, layer about 1 cup of the bean mixture, followed by one tortilla and ⅓ cup of cheese. Repeat these layers five times, finishing with cheese on top. Cover the Ninja Foodi PossibleCooker and cook on low for 4 to 5 hours, or until heated through and the cheese is melted. 4. Once cooked, use the foil strips as handles to carefully lift the pie out of the Ninja Foodi PossibleCooker and transfer it to a platter for serving. Enjoy!

Very Best Barbecue Beef Sandwiches

Prep time: 20 minutes | Cook time: 8 hours | Serves 12

- 1 (3- to 4-pound / 1.4- to 1.8-kg) boneless beef chuck roast
- 1½ cups ketchup
- 1 small onion, finely chopped
- ¼ cup packed brown sugar
- ¼ cup red wine vinegar
- 1 tablespoon Dijon mustard
- 1 tablespoon Worcestershire
- sauce
- 2 garlic cloves, minced
- ½ teaspoon salt
- ¼ teaspoon celery seed
- ¼ teaspoon paprika
- ¼ teaspoon pepper
- 2 tablespoons cornstarch
- 2 tablespoons cold water
- 12 kaiser rolls, split
- Dill pickle slices (optional)

1. Cut the roast in half and place it in a 5-quart Ninja Foodi PossibleCooker. In a small bowl, mix together the ketchup, chopped onion, brown sugar, vinegar, mustard, Worcestershire sauce, minced garlic, salt, celery seed, paprika, and black pepper. Pour this mixture over the roast. Cover and cook on low for 8 to 10 hours, or until the meat is tender. 2. Once cooked, carefully remove the meat from the Ninja Foodi PossibleCooker. Skim any fat from the cooking juices and transfer the juices to a large saucepan. Bring the juices to a boil. In a separate bowl, combine the cornstarch and water until smooth; then gradually stir this mixture into the boiling juices. Return to a boil and cook for 2 minutes, or until thickened. 3. When the meat is cool enough to handle, shred it using two forks. Return the shredded meat to the Ninja Foodi PossibleCooker and stir in the thickened sauce mixture, heating through. 4. Serve the meat on rolls, adding pickle slices if desired. Enjoy!

Appendix 1: Measurement Conversion Chart

VOLUME EQUIVALENTS(DRY)

US STANDARD	METRIC (APPROXIMATE)
1/8 teaspoon	0.5 mL
1/4 teaspoon	1 mL
1/2 teaspoon	2 mL
3/4 teaspoon	4 mL
1 teaspoon	5 mL
1 tablespoon	15 mL
1/4 cup	59 mL
1/2 cup	118 mL
3/4 cup	177 mL
1 cup	235 mL
2 cups	475 mL
3 cups	700 mL
4 cups	1 L

VOLUME EQUIVALENTS(LIQUID)

US STANDARD	US STANDARD (OUNCES)	METRIC (APPROXIMATE)
2 tablespoons	1 fl.oz.	30 mL
1/4 cup	2 fl.oz.	60 mL
1/2 cup	4 fl.oz.	120 mL
1 cup	8 fl.oz.	240 mL
1 1/2 cup	12 fl.oz.	355 mL
2 cups or 1 pint	16 fl.oz.	475 mL
4 cups or 1 quart	32 fl.oz.	1 L
1 gallon	128 fl.oz.	4 L

TEMPERATURES EQUIVALENTS

FAHRENHEIT(F)	CELSIUS(C) (APPROXIMATE)
225 °F	107 °C
250 °F	120 °C
275 °F	135 °C
300 °F	150 °C
325 °F	160 °C
350 °F	180 °C
375 °F	190 °C
400 °F	205 °C
425 °F	220 °C
450 °F	235 °C
475 °F	245 °C
500 °F	260 °C

WEIGHT EQUIVALENTS

US STANDARD	METRIC (APPROXIMATE)
1 ounce	28 g
2 ounces	57 g
5 ounces	142 g
10 ounces	284 g
15 ounces	425 g
16 ounces (1 pound)	455 g
1.5 pounds	680 g
2 pounds	907 g

Appendix 2: Recipes Index

Made in the USA
Las Vegas, NV
12 December 2024

13999348R00052